Tacitus Hussey

The River Bend

And Other Poems

Tacitus Hussey

The River Bend
And Other Poems

ISBN/EAN: 9783744709552

Printed in Europe, USA, Canada, Australia, Japan

Cover: Foto ©Thomas Meinert / pixelio.de

More available books at **www.hansebooks.com**

THE RIVER BEND

.... AND ....

OTHER POEMS

BY

TACITUS HUSSEY

ILLUSTRATED.

DES MOINES, IOWA:
CARTER & HUSSEY, PRINTERS.
1896.

.

CONTENTS.

Frontispiece, ... 2
Illustrations, ... 10
Proem, ... 11
Dedicatory, ... 13
The River Bend, ... 17
To Robin Redbreast, ... 20
The Reason Why, ... 21
The Hoosier Nectar, ... 22
The Summer's Farewell, ... 24
Disillusion, ... 25
High Lights, ... 26
When the Bloom Is on the Corn, ... 28
Chrysanthemum, ... 30
Our Hoosier State, ... 31
In Memory of J. Addison Hepburn, ... 32
My Lady's Violin, ... 33
June, ... 35
Memory's Cadence, ... 36
Till Death Do Us Part, ... 42
Junior Hymn, ... 43
The First Snow of Winter, ... 44
Early Called, ... 45
When the Mists Have Passed, ... 46
To Henry Watterson, ... 47
The Old Hawkeye Band, ... 48
The Friend in Need, ... 50
Vernal Longings, ... 54

Easter Day. 56
A Dream. 57
The Family Thought. 59
General James M. Tuttle. 60
In Memoriam. 62
July. 63
To Margaret. 64
Free Currency. 65
Christmas Bells. 67
You Know It. 70
Misapprehension. 71
Thanksgiving Suggestion. 72
Lovely May. 74
The Flood — 1892. 75
The Sunday School's Farewell. 77
Precaution. 79
The Kicker's Funeral. 80
Return of the Prodigals. 82
America's Crown. 87
To a November Dandelion. 88
A Surprise. 89
Memory's Song. 90
Hoosier Echoes. 91
Rising Genius. 93
Jubilee Year. 94
A Spring Beauty. 96
The Good Old Times. 99
Easter Morning. 101
Christmas. 102
The Poet's Plea. 103
Spring. 105
Goin' to Farmin'. 106
Tears Mingled. 108
Columbus Day. 109
The Tariff. 111

Christmas Carol. 112
Would Like Another Chance. 114
The Old Rain Barrel. 116
Prosperity. 118
The Temple Beautiful. 119
Which ? 121
A Thanksgiving Toast. 122
The Round Up. 123
The Homesick Hoosier. 124
The Under Cat, ... 128
Plain Jane and Me. 130
October, ... 132
The World's Fair Poem. 133
The Reluctant Idea. 135
The Race at Cherokee. 136
Forty Years in Iowa. 139
She Had. 141
Hoosier Recollections. 142
September. 144
Christmas Doings. 145
Reconsideration. 148
The Poet of the Future. 149
Cause and Effect. 151
A River Idyl. 155

POEMS ILLUSTRATED.

The River Bend,	Photos, H. N. Little,	Zeese & Sons, Engravers,
The Flood,	" "	" "
The Friend in Need,	" "	" "
Spring Beauty,	" "	" "
My Lady's Violin,	" F. W. Webster,	" "
Frontispiece, (The Author.)	" "	" "
Easter Day,	Illustration, Jennie Girton, Waterloo, Iowa,	
		Zeese & Sons, Engravers.
Dedicatory,	Photo, Ideal Portrait Co.,	" "
Forty Years in Iowa,	(Snap Shot,) F. H. Luthe,	" "
Christmas Bells,	Illustrations, Clara Hendricks,	Star Engraving Co.
Homesick Hoosier,	" "	'
Christmas Carol	" "	"
Return of the Prodigals,	" "	"

The press work on this book was done by courtesy of the Kenyon Printing and Manufacturing Company.

PROEM.

I saw a spider spin a slender thread,
  From his small spinaret, floating free ;
How busily he wrought, as on it sped —
  I stood and wondered what his aim could be.

And from his lowly workshop on the ground,
  Breeze-wafted, his tiny line rose higher,
And, fast'ning to a loftier shrub, he found
  By climbing, he could win his heart's desire.

                    .

Then, from the higher vantage ground, spun he,
  A longer thread, which soared high in the air,
And, wind-directed, touched a tall oak tree,
  Which caught it tenderly, and held it there.

So, like the spider, I have flung some lines
  Out on an unknown world, maybe, for naught ;
But trembling, hope that — if your heart inclines —
  You'll be the Oak, on which they've firmly caught !

DEDICATORY.

To her, who through life's sun and
    shade,
  In summer's heat, in winter's cold,
Since paths together have been laid
    To walk, until Life's tale is told ;
To her, the true and loving wife,
  Whose presence brightened many
    a mile
Upon the tortuous way of life,
  Who always met me with a smile.

The storm which swept Life's ocean, where
  Our little bark, at anchor lay,
Oft rudely stirred the waters there,
  In our snug harbor, " Sunshine Bay."
And clouds, which o'er our pathway wept,
  Their silver lining showed, the while ;
And shimmering through, the sunshine crept,
  Whene'er she met me with a smile.

So, all along the milestone's mark,
  Which separates the weary years,
The pilgrims trudge, in light or dark,
  Beset without, within, with fears ;
But oh ! the cloud-rifts on the way,
  Which many dreary hours beguile,
If he, at journey's end, can say :
" She always met me with a smile ! "

13

THE RIVER BEND
AND OTHER POEMS

THE RIVER BEND.

What joy, upon the dancing stream,
    Under the sweeping paddle's play,
'Neath tinted sky from sunset's gleam,
Where water-lilies lie and dream,
    Awaiting the soft touch of day,
To voyage in a light canoe,
    In which there's only room for two!

Where purling streams wind in and out,
 In wastefulness and wanton glee,
Where willows dip their thirsty boughs.
And lovers 'change undying vows
 Beneath the well known trysting tree.
We linger in our light canoe,
 In which there's only room for two!

The robin sings; or sweet brown thrush
 On topmost bough in evening air,
With heaving breast and swelling throat
Pours out his heart with every note;
 The while, we sit in silence there,
Concealed from the musician's view,
 Entranced, within the light canoe:

Or idly float, 'neath silent stars,
 While sprinkled thickly on the stream
Their bright reflected faces show;
With stars above and stars below,
 It all seems like a passing dream.
With thoughts too deep for words, we two
 Sit voiceless, in our light canoe!

Oh, Golden Silence! When two hearts
 Are throbbing with responsive beat!
When trembling on the lips are hung
The sweetest words of mortal tongue,
 Which lovers falt'ringly repeat:
" I love you!" who would not be true
 To plighted troth in light canoe?

Dear River Bend, with light and shade!
　　With fringed willows by the score,
Festooned with wild grape blossoms sweet,
While lipping waves thy name repeat
　　In whispered ripples 'long the shore;
Sad day, when we shall bid adieu
　　　To thee, and to our swift canoe!

And when down Life's long stream we glide
　　To where Styx' waters darkly roll,
And meet old Charon, gaunt and grim,
To his demandings say to him:
　"Insist not on our paying toll;
For, if it's just the same to you,
　　We'll cross o'er in our staunch canoe!"

TO ROBIN REDBREAST.

Old Winter, thou art going !
Sayest thou so, thou bird with breast of fiery red ;
Speakest thou as a prophet, or dost thou only guess ?
　　Art thou, then, so knowing ?

There may be frosts and snows
Ere the tongues of the little rills are loosed again,
And they joy to run the race with rivers to the sea ;
　　Who but the prophet, knows ?

When autumn leaves grew dry
And thou and thy mates looked on each other,
Saying in a language plainly understood :
　　" Why sit we here and die,

" When in Egypt there is food,
Where, in balmy air, perennial blooms the rose ;
Where snow and chilling frost, with biting icy breath
　　Can ne'er be understood ? "

O'er lakes and forests tall,
How foundest thou the way, by night, by day, in
Weary, toilsome flight, unless He did guide thee,
　　Who marks the sparrow's fall ?

Oh, happy wert thou then,
Bathing in the limpid stream and sunlight
With thy mate. Didst not thy heart often yearn
　　For thy north home again ?

Yes, I know it must, for see,
Thou art here, looking for the dear, familiar spots
Thou didst know and love last year. Even
　　The very apple tree,

Where thou and thy loved mate
Reared in safety, 'mid its sheltering branches,
A brood of five open-mouthed, callow fledglings
    To robin's full estate.

Thy song is very sweet
On evening air at set of sun. The new born day
Finds thee still praising Him who loves and cares for
    All his creatures. It is mete.

Prophetic, art thou, bird !
Thy presence brings visions of swelling buds, wild
Flowers, by King Winter's reign entombed, till Spring's
    Enchanting voice is heard ;

Nature's resurrection day ;
When the dead shall hear the voice : "Come forth again
Be warmed to life by summer's sun and shower ! "
    And joyfully obey.

THE REASON WHY.

" You naughty, wicked boy ! " she said,
    " To kill those pretty birds !
    I've half a mind--" her eyes flashed fire,
        More dangerous than her words.
" Please, miss," the frightened boy replied,
    . Cowering where he sat ;
" I had to kill these Orioles
        To trim my sister's hat ! "

THE HOOSIER NECTAR.

The spring is kinder lingerin'
  In Winter's lap they say,
Though the wild geese go a honkin' north
  An' the birds hev come to stay;
Yet there's an achin' void which can't
  Be filled by birds or grass
A hankerin' of the soul which cries
  For tea of Sassafras.

I jest set down sometimes and long
  For them Indiana woods,
When we uster, in the early days,
  Git purifyin' moods;
And usher in the early spring,
  Singly, or en masse,
By washin' down our corn pone bread
  With tea of Sassafras.

We'd never heerd of microbes then,
  In fact, they wasn't known;
The wisest doctors in the land
  Had never yet been shown
Such things as we are findin' now
  With magnifyin' glass
But they can all be driven out
  With tea of Sassafras.

It's jest too bad, Mirandy says,
  That she can't fer a minnit
Set out doors a pan of jelly
  'Thout them critters gittin' in it;
An' you git 'em in your system
  Jest by eatin' of this sass
An' to git 'em out we hev to drink
  The tea of Sassafras!

Pennyroyal may be fairly good,
　Er Boneset, to the taste,
But drinkin' store tea in the spring
　Is only jest a waste;
Ef you want ter purify yer blood,
　An' avoid too much "blue mass,"
Jest grab a grubbin' hoe and dig
　Some roots of Sassafras

An' bile 'em fer a spell, and drink
　The tea three times a day,
An' the megrums and blue devils
　Will forever flee away.
There comes a time in all our lives
　When the heavens are as brass,
An' blood corp'sules jest holler out
　For tea of Sassafras!

Some men spend nearly all their lives
　At colleges and sich,
To dig out roots with skeery names
　That haint no use, and which
Are used to mystify and skeer
　The ignoranter class,
Who jest go on from spring to spring,
　Drinkin' tea of Sassafras!

We allus brew some of this tea,
　In spring twilight, soft and dim.
An' git the old blue teapot out
　An' fill it to the brim;
Then set and quaff this beverage
　Until we gently pass
In sweet dreams, to Indianny, with
　Her tea of Sassafras!

THE SUMMER'S FAREWELL.

Dying:

Summer with her birds and flowers ;
  Leaves with blood-red colors glinting
  In the smoke veiled sun's soft tinting :
  To regretful mortals hinting.
Death to summer shine and showers.
      Slowly dying !

Fading:

How the summer flowers are fading !
  There yet remains the goldenrod
  To greet the world with graceful nod.
  Its sweet face lifted up to God.
With answering tints of sunset's shading.
      Sweetly lingering !

Flitting:

See how summer birds are flocking.
  For the warm south home's returning :
  Knowing well and well discerning
  Warmth and food there waits the earning.
Where Nature's door opes to their knocking.
      Happy songsters !

Chafing:

Ah, my soul, what a glad winging !
  Breaking cords of care and toiling
  Hands and hearts forever soiling.
  Flying far from labor's moiling.
To fill the earth and air with singing !
      Life's unchaining !

Passing:
Like the summer. life is passing!
    How. like changing leaf of myrtle
    Fade we, fall and pass the portal
    Leading to the life immortal,
Where the King of Life is sitting!
        Swiftly passing!

DISILLUSION.

Her eyes were of the deepest blue.
    Her teeth were white as pearls;
My heart beat at a furious rate;
My eyes were fastened to my plate;
My ego said: "She is your fate
    This prettiest of girls!"
And when she raised her face to mine.
    What sweetness filled my cup!
But when with ear of corn between
Her lily hands were toying seen,
She gnawed the rows off, slick and clean,
    I sighed and gave her up!

HIGH LIGHTS.

Last evenin' I was left alone and kinder fell to musin'
   'Bout them times when all the world was sort o' slow and shore ;
When the days were meant for work, and the nights were used
     for snoozin',
   And the latch-string used to hang from everybody's door.

How we used to ride to church in any sort of weather
   Behind a patient ox team, with a jolly lot of pairs,
Who warn't never in a hurry and did not care much whether
   They got there just in time for first or second prayers.

There's no such thing as hurry and 'twas little use to bother
   An ox team as it took its way from early morn till night;
But the delib'rate way they put one foot before the other,
   To a man of moderation was a very restful sight.

I seemed to see before me, my cabin wall's adornin',
   The strips of pumpkin dryin', with Calamus and Sage,
The Pennyroyal, Boneset, Tansy and the dry seed corn in
   Rows, for the spring seedin', and the Catnip for tender age.

The plates up in the cupboard all set on aige and gleamin'
   In the light from open fire, in the fire place, big and wide,
The dancin' shadders on the walls, the tea-kittle a steamin',
   The backlog throwing sparkles out the andirons beside.

That the world is makin' changes is not to be disputed,
   But if you jest could see the sights I witness every day,
You'd wonder jest as I do, how sech High Art evoluted,
   An' got tangled up with Bricky-brack in such a skeery way.

Our Sunday wash-rags all have got a Jaberwock a starin',
  My boot-jack is a pinchin'-bug, with wild, protrudin' eyes,
With Griffins on the wash-bowl, while the pitcher is a sharin'
  The deep glow of one of Italy's most excited skies!

I eat my fish on Fridays from one of those hand-wrought dishes,
  With a pickerel painted on it, jest a gaspin' for its breath,
While the butterflies, the millers, and the thirsty little fishes
  'Round the aige, give silent witness to its very cruel death.

Mirandy says the painters in the medieval ages
  Worked long upon their picters for they'd nothin' else to do
An' descanted 'bout sech art on history's future pages
  While I sewed on a button fer to hitch my gallus to!

An' as fer taking lessons, folks don't think of sech a thing;
  They jest git brush and canvas and paint picters on the run
And pester old Dame Natur' or shoot her on the wing
  With the ever-present Kodack, or the photographic gun!

Then there's Extension Lecters, plain people's thoughts beguilin'.
  And leading their ambition and intellect astray,
By 'Varsity Professors, jest to keep their pots a bilin',
  Which may be would be difficult in any other way.

And women in the sixties, doin' Delsartean acts,
  An' imitatin' antics which our frisky maidens do ;
And tryin to be graceful at expense of achin' backs
  Land of hope and blessed promise! What's the world a comin'
    to ?

WHEN THE BLOOM IS ON THE CORN.

When the goldenrod is budding
  On the hills and by the streams,
As an earnest that it soon will glad
  Our eyes with sunny beams ;
When the katydid persistent sings
  From early eve till morn,
All nature seems to joy with us
  When the bloom is on the corn.

The goldenrod with nodding plumes
  In every waste place grows :
The katydid, in thrilling tones,
  Pipes the only song it knows :
Æsthetic people, at these two,
  May curl their lip in scorn ;
But flower and song are dear to me,
  As the bloom upon the corn.

I sit me down sometimes and long
  For those bright fabled lands,
Where sweet perennial roses bloom
  'Mid billowy waste of sands,
But content myself with wondering
  If it would not be forlorn
Ne'er to mix those sweet breathed flowers
  With the bloom upon the corn.

And oh, when Want or Famine, sore,
  Rears up its famished head ;
While children tug at mother's skirts
  With hungry cries for bread ;
How sweet 'twill be to still those cries,
  Across the waters borne,
By sending them relief, because
  The bloom is on the corn.

If all the plants, excepting corn,
  Were compressed into one,
For crowning of the king of earth,
  For the good that he had done,
King Maize would then be laurel wreathed,
  And proudly would be worn,
Amid the plaudits of the world,
  While the bloom is on the corn.

Proud Iowa, with flowers bedecked,
  As fair as any bride,
To thee I sing this simple strain,
  With a heart uplift of pride.
As nations turn their eyes to thee,
  Their children yet unborn
Will bless thee, with uplifted hands,
  For the bloom upon the corn.

CHRYSANTHEMUM.

She peeps at me through the window pane
    As I pass with lingering pace;
How sweet she looks, but does not deign
To invite the touch which I would fain
    Place on her witching face.
How fair she is in her dainty dress,
    And wherefore is she come,
In winter season thus to bless
Us with her blooming? Can you guess
    Her name? Chrysanthemum!

How sweet of her, when the year is old,
    With the breath of frost and ice,
To link the seasons, warm and cold,
With floral chain of red and gold,
    Of Nature's own device!
Oh, queen, well worthy of a crown!
    To teach us thou art come.
To give brightness for a winter's frown;
Thus smiling all despondence down,
    Like thee, Chrysanthemum!

OUR HOOSIER STATE.

We sing the Hoosier's glad refrain
In joying that we meet again,
To sing a song and shake the hánd
In memory of our native land.
    Oh, Hoosier Land, Loved Hoosier Land,
    With r vers, lakes and forests grand;
Our thoughts are turning back to thee,
And in our vision still can see
The old well sweep, the cabins low,
Our happy homes of long ago.

Our thoughts go roaming through the glade,
And rest at times beneath the shade
Of Paw Paw tree, or spreading Linn,
The sweet Black Haw or Chinquapin.
    Oh, Hoosier Land, Loved Hoosier Land.
    Thy visions rise on every hand;
We ride again, with little joy;
Along thy roads of Corduroy,
And drink, without a trace of smile,
Thy Boneset tea in every style!

Dear Hoosier State, our memory's pride,
We love thee, laying jokes aside,
We crown thy memory to-day
With wreaths of Dogwood blossoms gay.
    Oh, Hoosier Land, Loved Hoosier Land;
    We for thy honor ever stand;
We'll ne'er forget the taste or smell
Of Sassafras and Calomel;
We'll drink thy health without remark
In Whisky mixed with Cherry Bark '

IN MEMORY OF J. ADDISON HEPBURN.

Folded hands, now white and still,
  Silently surrendering
All to God's most gracious will ;
Gone, beyond all care and ill,
  Dust to dust now rendering ;
      Folded, placid hands,
      Once such busy hands.

What to them life's busy throng
  From it now dismembering ?
He, whose life was as a song ;
A heart which carolled all day long,
  With notes well worth remembering.
      Folded, icy hands.
      Once such clinging hands.

Folded hands, now sweet in rest,
  Friendship's strong ties sundering,
Feeling that God knoweth best.
Consenting to His high behest.
  Weeping still and wondering :
      Folded, idle hands,
      Empty, trusting hands.

Folded, tired and weary hands,
  Quietly and trustingly,
Waiting the Father's loved commands.
To rise to sun-kissed upper lands,
  In peace the Savior's face to see ;
      Promise grasping hands,
      Happy, clinging hands.

MY LADY'S VIOLIN.

If I were but her violin,
Resting beneath her dimpled chin,
  How happy would I be?
With fingers pressing here and there,
Gliding in cadence everywhere,
With touches light and passing fair,
  That would be heaven for me,
    If I were but her violin,
    Her soul-entrancing violin !

If I were but her violin,
Resting beneath her snow-white chin,
  What could I want beside !
With fingers fair by her caressed,
Reposing on her heaving breast,
Like chirping birdling in its nest,
  Could there a woe betide.
    If I were but her violin,
    Her spirit-soothing violin ?

If I were but her violin,
Pressed lightly by her rounded chin,
  How silent would I lie !
Waiting the touch of magic bow,
Wielded by arm as white as snow,
Giving me voice, now loud. now low.
  In sweetest melody,
    If I were but her violin,
    Her foot-bewitching violin !

If I were but her violin,
Pressed lovingly beneath her .chin,
  Ah, what ecstatic bliss !
To feel the throbbing of each vein,
As from sweet music's tangled skein
Come sounds as soft as summer's rain.
  When storm clouds gently kiss ;
    If I were but her violin,
    Her wooing, cooing violin !

If I were but her violin,
With envied place beneath her chin.
  How sweet would be the note
I'd yield to her caressing hands.
The treasure which her skill demands :
Or, servile be. as slave who stands
  To kiss the hand which smote,
    If I were but her violin,
    Her heart-subduing violin !

If I were but her violin,
To rest no more beneath her chin,
    How sad would be the day
When Music's daughter was brought low,
And when, with trembling hands and slow,
She'd lay me, with the useless bow,
    Forever from her touch away !
        An old, neglected violin,
        A silent, soundless violin !

JUNE.

Oh, month of dainty roses !
    Brought forth by warm May showers,
We hail thee with thy garlands
    Of gaily tinted flowers.
But there's a dark suspicion
    That thy glories without doubt,
In charming Nature's lovers,
    Will hatch the microbes out !

MEMORY'S CADENCES.

Read before Early Settlers Society, September 13, 1892.

Do you ask why this infliction,
Why I sing this song before you,
Filled with very ancient legends,
Bringing back to fading memories
Incidents almost forgotten,
Even many jokes with whiskers?
Listen, I will quickly tell you,
Why, from mind so retrospective.
I have sown beside all waters,
Reaping now a memory's harvest:
Listen, you will all remember,
That, in an unguarded moment,
You elected me historian,
Hence, you'll have to grin and bear it!

Whence gained I these musty mouthings
With the moss of age upon them,
With the odor of the forests
Mingling with the prairie flowers;
Just as nature breathed upon them
In our then primeval forests,
On our boundless, trackless prairies?

I will tell you if you'll hearken
Barlow Granger taught me many,
By his Star, which rose in splendor,
In the year before the fifties,

When he printed in a cabin
The first paper in this section ;
Fighting cold in dead of winter,
Which crept through the interstices.
By live coals beneath his presses,
Thus to soften ink and rollers.
Honor be to Barlow Granger,
For his Star, thus early shining,
Lightened up the settler's pathway :
Spoke our village into being !
Honor be to L. P. Sherman,
Who, by his Gazette has taught me
Many stories of privations
He endured in eighteen fifty,
When he ate his bread with scarceness,
Sharing with his poorer neighbors ;
Honors thrice to L. P. Sherman !
Learned them in the settler's cabins
At their frugal dinner tables,
Eating corn pone without butter,
Spearing bacon from the skillet
Where it swam in richest gravy !
Ah, those times of want and scarceness,
How they welded hearts together
In a way not soon forgotten !

George G. Wright, the story teller,
The just Judge from Keosauqua,
He has told me many stories,
Mixing up my tears with laughter !

You remember Martin Tucker,
Who had " stabling at right angles."
On his tavern built " condition."

Ran an "avenue" through the middle,
"Detained" guests in "hostile" manner?
And Squire Young, the thoughtful student,
Drove a nail in floating pontoon,
At the water's edge he drove it,
In the evening, at the "Float Bridge,"
Thus to note the rising water.
In the morning, though the river
Looked more angry and seemed wider,
He declared it had not risen
By the tell-tale nail's position!
And the jovial Billy Woodwell,
Once, when east to buy some hardware,
Loaded up a boat with grindstones.
Thus he argued to his partners: —
"Every one must have a grindstone;
Rich and poor of every station
Needs one of these circular sharpeners
What is life, without a grindstone?
We must boom the grindstone business!"

Billy Moore, the old-time druggist,
Drifting into dry goods, notions,
Hats and caps and ladies' bonnets,
Had his store oft filled with buyers;
By his genial disposition,
By his long old-time acquaintance,
By the tremor of his eyelids,
Winked them out of lots of money!

When the spring unlocked the rivers
From old Winter's icy fetters,
When the wild goose flying northward
Hinted at the coming springtime,

Visions brought of birds and violets ;
Then there came a sound far sweeter,
Listened for by anxious settlers ;
Looked for with intensest longing.
Far adown the rapid river
Came a sound of prolonged harshness,
Somewhat softened by the distance,
Told the coming of a steamboat - ·
First arrival of the season !
Babes were left in cradles sleeping,
Stores and offices deserted,
Men in haste, with hair disheveled,
Women, with sunbonnets swinging,
Sometimes without shoes or stockings,
Sped with hastening feet to landing,
Glad to meet the new arrival,
Six days from the Mississippi.
Linking us to civilization !
Ah, the comforts they have brought us,
Rice and sugar, flour and bacon,
Tea and coffee, drugs and dry goods,
Hardware, millinery—whisky !
How the men all eyed those barrels ·
Longed to taste their fiery contents ;
How the women longed for bonnets !
Wondered if they'd be becoming !

Names of boats you fain would ask me :
Here they are, from memory's storehouse
See if you can recognize them :
The lone that brought the soldiers ;
Caleb Cope, Add Hine, Kentucky,
John B. Gordon, Globe, Luella,
Clara Hine and Little Morgan,

Des Moines Belle and Charlie Rodgers.
Flora Temple, De Moine City,
Badger State, Nevada, Alice ;
And, no doubt, there were some others,
Which have slipped from cells of memory.

You remember Isaac Cooper,
Energetic early settler,
Dug the first well in this county,
Using as a tool a skillet ;
Made the first shoes in this township,
From boot legs and skirt of saddle,
Becoming, thus, the first " bootlegger."

Ezra Rathburn, the first preacher,
Gave first sermon in this section,
Followed soon by many others.
Thompson Bird, of blessed memory,
Broke the Bread of Life in cabins,
Trudged on foot to meet appointments,
Sometimes swam his horse through rivers ;
His was love that waters quenched not,
For his heart ne'er ceased its singing ;
His was zeal that darkness dimmed not,
For his lamp was trimmed and burning.
J. A. Nash, the much lamented,
He, the loved of everybody,
Founded the first Baptist mission,
In the great flood year of Iowa,
Eighteen fifty-one, when rivers
Swelled by rains in torrents falling,
Crept beyond the banks' confining,
Flooded all the river's lowlands !

Should you ask a Baptist brother
Of this year of tribulation,
If, between this flood and founding,
There was any real connection,
He a pitying look will give you.
But no word will give in answer.

Let the names of early settlers
E'er be wreathed in brightest laurels ;
Let their memories be cherished :
Tears for dead and cheers for living.
They have smoothed life's rugged pathway
For the coming feet of children ;
They have laid a good foundation
Broad and deep, for coming thousands
Who will tread these fruitful valleys,
When the Old World, gaunt and hungry,
Turns her longing eyes to Iowa,
Land of corn, wheat, milk and honey,
Kissed of God, by sun and shower !

Golden, shining links of friendship,
Welded by half century's forgings,
In the time when Want and Scarceness
Were unbidden guests at firesides,
Year by year are being broken.
Like the tinted leaves of Autumn
When the soft wind breathes upon them,
They are falling.   They are passing
To the " House of Many Mansions ! "

Thus we sing a song of gladness.
Mingled with regrets and sorrow.
For the many missing faces

Which were wont to mingle with us ;
Joying in the glad possessions
They have left to living children.

There is still an old tradition
Reaching back into the ages,
That our Iowa, in creation
Was the happy Eden Garden,
Where, in summer, our first parents
Walked this land in airy costume.
Isaac Brandt told me this story
Years ago, when these broad prairies
Caused his heart to throb with pleasure ;
Charmed the eye of all beholders.
I believe this sweet tradition.
I believe by excavation
In the soil, so richly laden
With the food for every nation,
We may find the bones of Adam !

TILL DEATH DO US PART.

" Where are you going, young man," she said,
    " With pistol at your side ? "
" I am going to ask a fair young girl
    To be my bonnie bride ! "
" Suppose she refuse," the maiden said ;
    Then he tapped his belt of leather ;
" Should she decline with thanks, we'll climb
    The Golden Stairs together ! "

JUNIOR HYMN.

Oh, God, we lift our hearts to Thee,
    A little praying band,
To Thee, the source of every good,
    Oh, lead us by the hand,
And teach us, by Thy love so free,
That boys and girls may trust in Thee.

We come with youthful hearts to-day
    To sing Thy songs of praise;
To Thee, our father's God to Thee
    Our earnest voices raise,
And ask that Thou, o'er all this land
Will bless the Junior C. E. Band.

As bows the tender mother's ear
    To catch the prattler's word,
Sweeter to her than any sound
    By which her heart is stirred,
So may the Savior's heart, to-day,
Be gladdened while the Juniors pray.

Oh, Thou, the source of life and light,
    We raise our thoughts to Thee;
Lead Thou us on, in works of love,
    'Till we Thy face shall see.
Then shall we see, and hear, and know,
Why God the Father loves us so.

THE FIRST SNOW OF WINTER.

Whirling and swirling the snow comes down ;
  Beautiful snow with its crystals pure,
Covering valleys and forests brown,
Unsightly streets of country - and town.
The first intimation of winter's frown,
  The joy of the rich, the dread of the poor ;
Oh, cruel snow, with flakes so white,
Thou art falling on her grave to-night !

Silently, softly, the cold flakes heap,
  Fighting for place on the wintry ground ;
Shrouding the graves where the flowers sleep,
Drifting on plain and rocky steep
In many a curious shape and heap,
  Covering the old and new made mound.
Oh, winter's snow, with veil so white,
Thou art resting on his grave to-night !

In open fire upon the tiled hearth
  Come forms and images of the misty past,
And trooping forth comes sharers of the mirth
In years behind you, when the whole round earth
Seemed all of joy, and came no dearth,
  Nor shadow on your happiness was cast ;
Nor could you say of hope's young blight,
The snow is falling on its grave to-night !

Dying are the coals within the grate,
  Anon the ashes through the bars are cast,
Their lives consumed. Such is the fate
Of those who live for others, and who wait
With patience, born of trust, the future state,
  Where Peace and Joy review the shadowy past,
With heart cries stilled, nor chill afright,
Of winter's snow upon the graves at night !

EARLY CALLED.

Very handsome
Young man, he ;
Father rich as
Rich could be.
Lucky chappie !

Smoked cigarettes
Day and night ;
Air tight casket,
" Out of sight."
Weeping parents.
When men die for want of sense,
We sobbing, whisper, " Providence ! "

WHEN THE MISTS HAVE PASSED.

For now we see through a glass, darkly.—1. Cor. xiii, 12.

How we grope and blindly wander,
  As we pass life's journey through ;
Judging men and women harshly
  In so many things they do ;
For our vision is so darkened
  By the veil which hides the day,
Till the sun shall rise in splendor
  And the mists shall roll away.

Men we've marched with in life's conflict,
  Touching elbows in the line,
Bivouacking on the battle fields,
  Kneeling at the self same shrine ;
But their hearts were veiled and hidden,
  From trusting friends for aye,
And whose love for them will brighten
  When the mists have passed away.

There are men in humble stations,
  Toiling for their daily food ;
We oft pass them by with coldness ;
  They are not understood.
Bye and bye, when we shall see them
  In the sunlight, we shall say :
" Would that we had known you better,
  Ere the mists had cleared away."

When our wealth is weighed in balance.
How strange will be the sight,
That the fortune of the miser
Don't outweigh the widow's mite ;
When a cup of water given,
In a gentle, loving way,
Will bring joy unto the giver,
When the mists have passed away !

TO HENRY WATTERSON.

Ah, Watterson. you brave old boy !
We're glad the war is over ;
And now the North and South will live
In harmony and clover ;
We'll nevermore go round with chips
Perched on defiant shoulder ;
Nor let the hate of North or South
Within our bosoms smoulder.
God bless our Henry Watterson,
For his patriotic story !
Three cheers for our New North and South,
And a " Tiger " for " Old Glory ! "

THE OLD HAWKEYE BAND.

Respectfully dedicated to the survivors of 1860.

Your big State Band is awful nice :
    Its music is jest grand ;
But you oughter heerd, in times gone by,
    The famous " Hawkeye Band."
Lor', there was harm'ny for the soul,
    And music fer the feet :
The verdick of them days was that
" Sech music's hard to beat ! "

A. Hartung was our leader,
    Ed. Kimball blowed the bass,
Billy Boyd the leadin' cornet.
    And Newt Curl the second place ;
Hutton, Carter, Houstons, Hussey,
    Bitting. Estabrook and Hoare.
With Sam Noble second Tuba,
    Made up the jolly corps.

Our clothes were not as fine as ther'n,
    Ner wore sech handsome caps,
All trimmed with brass and old gold lace
    And lined with silk. perhaps.
We wore our best no two alike
    Ner did we ever 'spose
The crowds which hung around, entranced,
    Hed come to see our clothes !

You'd oughter seen us fellers march
  Fust time, on a parade ;
Fer every man tuck his own time
  And acted kind o' 'fraid.
You see we wasn't used to sech ;
  And from fust man to twelfth,
He started out onto a gait
  Jest suited to hisself !

We had no big " Drum Major " man
  A whirlin' of a club
And a struttin' proudly on before
  To the drum's sharp " rub-a-dub."
We played the chunes to suit ourselfs
  With all our soul and mind,
And no one " guyed " a player ef
  He was a bar behind.

The chunes? Wall, you will think them old—
  To me they'll never die ;
The " Java March," the " Soldier's Joy,"
" Katy Darling," " Nellie Bly,"
" Massa's in the Cold, Cold Ground,"
  " The Long, Long Weary Day,"
The " Hawkeye Polka," " Polonaise,"
  And " Darling Nellie Gray."

Ah, well, I 'spose that everything
  In time will pass away ;
And every band, as well as dog,
  Must also hev their day ;
But if I am so fort'nate
  As to tramp the golden strand,
'Twill not be heaven at all to me
  Without that " Hawkeye Band ! "

COMODORE KELLY'S NAVY YARD

General Kelly's Industrial Army arrived in Des Moines, Sunday, April 29. 1894, and finding no means of transportation at hand built scows at the junction of Des Moines and Raccoon rivers and embarked on May 9, and continued their journey. The wives of some of the citizens joined the flotilla, but were sent back as soon as the fact became known to the Commodore. The "angels" alluded to were two women who joined the army at Council Bluffs, and shared its fortunes. They had state rooms on the "Flag Ship."

THE FRIEND IN NEED.

Bear them gently, bear them gently, dear river of Des Moines,
Down through our much loved Iowa, where your sparkling waters join
The Mississippi river, with its calm majestic sweep,
As it runs its race with patience to swell the vasty deep,
Where the ocean will receive it, send the waters back again
In soft, refreshing showers, to gladden Iowa's plain.

How sweet of you, dear river, when our folks began to shout
That " Kelly's hungry army had worn their welcome out ; "
When railroads, so aggressive and so fond of the " long haul,'
Would not even furnish " hog rates," — or any rates at all ;
How sweet of you, I say again, to bare your breast and say :
" Come, rest upon this bosom ! Accept this shining way ! "

Oh, sandbars ! Hide your faces now, and be ye water-veiled,
Until this fleet of working men have past your presence sailed ;
And snags, will you please clear the track and let the navy go,
Unhindered and untrammeled, on its winding way and slow?
Crab apple blossoms, when you can, perfume the gentle breeze.
To mingle with grape blossoms' scent — bow low, ye willow trees !

Be kind to them, oh, river ! Encourage them to think
That it's good for outside cleansing, as well as for a drink :
And shore sands, be ye softened, where the gentle river flows,
As the softest beds and pillows where the rich man may repose ;
And silver moon. unclouded. give them thy gentle ray,
That by sunlight and by moonlight, they may hasten on their
    way,

AL SWALM.

On the high and holy duty on which
    they say they're sent,
To shake the Tree of Fortune — and the
    General Government !
Don't delay them, little Eddyville, at your
    pretty horseshoe bend —
Fill them up with grub and move them
    on to their journey's end ;
Keep Al Swalm clean off the Flag Ship —
    lest to all our grief,
They should take him down to Washington as a captive Indian
    Chief !

This world can not be. equal made, no matter how we try ;
For some must eat the stale brown bread, while others " swipe
    the pie ! "
And it is not unnatural that the common tars should roar,
That " Kelly hugs the angels, while we have to hug the shore ! "
Ottumwa, why be timid ? Let General Kelley land
His fleet and take collection to the music of his band ;

His tars are very harmless -- you need not fear your lives
Leave your chicken coops wide open — but fasten up your wives !
I always thought 'twas uniforms which charmed a woman's gaze —
But brass buttons are " not in it " compared to pretty ways ;
For women are intuitive and maybe this is how
They see the noble purpose which wreaths each manly brow.

Keosauqua, give them welcome, with provisions without end —
They'll need it, these brave sailors, when they voyage round that
    bend
Of fourteen miles and over. Don't mention it, alack !
Lest they fear there is no ending and try to paddle back

Just pass them o'er those rapids, on, past old Bentonsport,
To the twelve foot dam at Bonaparte, for here there'll be some
    sport

In getting the fleet over. For the boys it will be fun ;
And it's altogether likely that there'll be more d– ns than one !
Then Farmington will pass the boys along the river fine,
And Missouri ·then will share the work of keeping them in line ;
Perhaps, too, in the way of feed, she'll lend a hand at that,
And while the glee club sings a song, Kelly will pass the hat.

Bear them oh, so gently, river sweet, let nothing interfere
To cause the men or " angels," to shed a single tear.
Oh, favoring winds !   Oh, current strong !   Bring to them all
    good luck,
And land them on the border line, four miles from Keokuk !

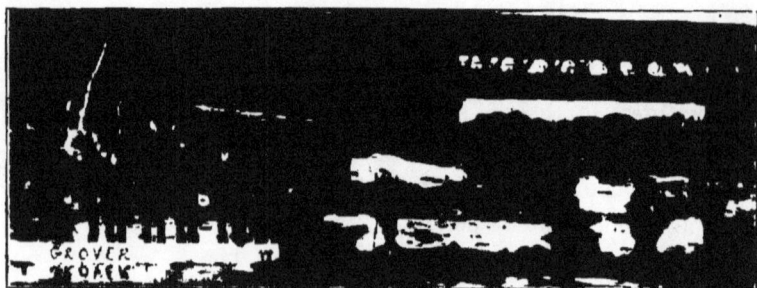

VERNAL LONGINGS.

It's yet a bit too early to plan for comin' spring,
   An' yet I'm gittin' anxious to see wild flowers once more,
A noddin' in the sunshine, while the bees upon the wing,
   Sip eagerly from morn till night the honey that they store
For winter's use, when storm clouds lower and frost is in the sky ;
   There's wisdom in jest sech a course, as it would seem to me —
Fer there's lots of us poor workin' folks a standin' idly by,
   Who wish now they had taken some pointers from the bee.

I'm hungerin' an' a thirstin' to hear the robin's note
   At sunset, on the topmost twig of his favorite elm tree ;
As he carols forth his gladness as to almost split his throat,
   Don't you think he could give pointers in praise to you an' me?
Whene'er I hear a robin sing, I allus have to smile
   At the earnest way he tackles it an' carries it along —
I haint so fond of music, yet I b'lieve I'd walk a mile
   To hear his " Peep-kuk-kill-'em-cure-'em-give-'em-physic " song.

I want to see the tender grass on sunny slopes a sproutin',
   An' comin' up to rest the eye from winter's robe of white.
An' hunt fer dandelion greens an' slowly walk about in
   Shirt sleeves - an' dream of bacon, which is my heart's delight ;
Er else set out of doors on the lee side of the woodpile
   An' watch the hens a scratchin', with their trim an' yeller legs,
With a sharp look out fer bugs ; an' I allus have a good smile
   As my thoughts mix with their cackle, of future ham an' eggs.

The hen, as I have sized her up, is a very honest bird ;
  Her voice has no great compass--but she has some pretty ways ;
An' of all the farmyard songsters that ever I have heard,
  I believe that I'm enamored, mostly, of her recent lays !
Just think of it ! Our Hawkeye hens, when busily at work,
  Increase our working capital a million, every year ;
She attends no " Hen Conventions " an' was never known to
    shirk,
  While she sings her modest anthems our hungry hearts to cheer.

Yes, I'm glad the winter's breakin' an' the wild goose north a
    flyin'
  In his harrow-shaped procession, marked on the softened sky.
An' hear the honkin' note as the day is slowly dyin',
  Tellin' us of flowin' rivers, as he passes slowly by.
Old Winter ! We'll forgive you, an' fergit your frosty pinchin'
  In the joy of your departure -- an' your later meltin' ways ;
An' our hearts beat high with hope of the pleasures we'll be
    sippin',
  When Nature, resurrected, joins us in a hymn of praise.

So I'm longin' fer the spring time, with a deep an' earnest long ;
  When winter's woes will fade away an' flowers take their place ;
When birds in woods and meadows, will cheer us with a song
  That will make us all fergit we've met Sorrow, face to face.
Old Earth is tipping to the south to meet the summer's sun ;
" Old Glory," with her starry folds, waves o'er our land to-day ;
Have faith in God the Father — and with each duty bravely done,
  We need fear no great disaster to our loved America.

h, Easter Day!

The swelling buds thy coming wait;
The puss willow with feath'ry fronds,
Lightly, in limpid streams and ponds
Dip eager boughs with joy elate:
      Oh, Easter Day!
      Dear Easter Day!

      Oh, Easter Day!
The violet blue, with eyes intent
Upon the shining track above,
Gazes with an unuttered love,
To mark the way our Savior went:
      Oh, Easter Day!
      Dear Easter Day!

A DREAM.

I had a funny dream last night —
  (I wonder if 'twas true ?)
It came in such a curious way,
  That I must tell it you.
An evening had been spent in bliss
  Among some maidens fair,
With sparkling eyes and rosy cheeks,
  And every shade of hair.

The time how spent, you ask, my friend,
  In such a jolly crowd?
" Progressive Euchre? " Guess again.
  " Whist? " " Conversation loud? "
Jaws moved at regular intervals
  'Tis true, but lips were dumb - -
From cherub mouths came not a sound —
  They all were chewing gum !

The girl I loved was in the throng,
  And soon I sought her out —
We walked amid the flowers and trees,
  ' And everywhere, about ;
I told her all my heart, and asked,
  " Will you my wife become ? "
She deeply sighed — she pressed my hand - -
  But kept on chewing gum !

" Joy of my heart ! " I said, at length,
  " Queen of my soul ! My pride !
Breathe in my ear the happy dav
  When you will be my bride ! "
I waited answer, while my heart
  Beat like a muffled drum :
She heaved an able-bodied sigh —
  And calmly chewed her gum !

" Oh, name the happy day ! " I cried.
  " And let me call thee mine ;
My fortune at thy feet I lay -
  I worship at thy shrine ! "
My fervor seemed to startle her,
  And, almost overcome,
I kissed her mantling cheek, while she
  Continued chewing gum !

  *   *   *   *   *

Oh, glorious day, that made me now
  So happy in my choice —
I answered all the questions plump --
  My heart was in my voice.
She nodded an assent to hers --
  The preacher was struck dumb —
I hardly could believe my eyes --
  She still was chewing gum !

  *   *   *   *   *

My dream then changed — it seemed to me
  That she had passed away
To that bright land, where sunshine holds
  An undisputed sway.
The vision brightened as I gazed
  Into the world to come —
Lo ! there she stood, with hand-picked saints,
  Forever chewing gum !

THE FAMILY THOUGHT,

A tear clung to her eyelids wet ;
  Her heart was all distraught—
She'd quarrelled with her husband, dear,
  These souls with single thought.
He wished the thought for base ball rules,
  And she, on the contrary,
Desired to use it for herself,
  In new style millinery ;
Thus, often is life's battle fought
By marrying without second thought !

GENERAL JAMES M. TUTTLE.

The hero calmly sleeps ;
Nor cannon's roar, nor music's sweetest breath
Can now disturb his slumbers, while his death
A nation sadly weeps.

Hero of Donelson,
Iowa, her tribute, lays upon thy grave ;
Her torn and war-stained banners wave
Over her fallen son !

Ah, that brave charge again,
At Donelson, while a world wondering stood
At the great gallantry and hardihood
Of Iowa's brave men.

Hope of the Nation they,
As through showers of leaden hail and shell,
Never men marched so bravely, nor so well,
As Second Iowa !

Up, higher ! Higher still,
Silently, but surely, they climb ! They mount
Where earthworks frown and Glory deeds recount,
Led by this hero's will.

First on the earthworks. Now
Cheering to deeds of valor thy brave men ;
Earthworks and glory won together, when
Victory crowned thy brow !

So long as sun upon
Our banner with stars undimmed, shall light
With glints and gleams, so shall thy memory be bright
Hero of Donelson !

IN MEMORIAM.

Respectfully dedicated to the Second Iowa Infantry.

Scatter flowers, beautiful flowers,
    On the graves
    Of the braves ;
Sleep they sweetly here, enbalmed by many tears ;
Whose brave deeds grow brighter with the passing years,
As higher on the scroll of fame each name appears,
    Written in blood.

Scatter flowers, choice spring flowers,
    Where they sleep,
    As we weep
Tears of gratitude to those who bravely wrought
Out a Nation's destiny ! How poor is thought
To tell the great blessing to a people fraught
    By such sacrifice.

Cover them with flowers, unfading flowers,
    O'er the head
    Of the dead ;
Dying, that no star upon our country's crest
Might be dimmed nor lost. Heeding the high behest,
That one flag should wave o'er North, South, East and West,
    Whate'er the cost !

Cover them with flowers — Immortelles ;
　　　For the dead tears,
　　　For the living, cheers ;
Ah, those heroes of Shiloh and Donelson,
Where waved first our flag on rebel earthworks won,
While a Nation watched, waiting to shout, " Well done,
　　　Brave boys in Blue ! "

Scatter choice flowers, Memory's flowers,
　　　Every May,
　　　In memory
Of those who, when called, counted life not dear,
But laid it gladly down without a fear ;
While our Nation lives, shall we not each year
　　　Bedeck their graves ?

JULY.

" Oh, July sun, let up, let up ;
　　Before you bake us brown,
　Or drive us to the lakes and woods,
　　Far, far away from town ! "
The sun said, with caloric smile :
" Come, listen now, my dears ;
If I don't work this month, what would
　You do for roasting ears ? "

TO MARGARET.

Merry, little dancing feet,
  Eyes with tint of heaven's blue,
With her little ways so sweet,
  Joyous all the long day through ;
Sometimes wayward, sometimes gay,
  As the notion takes my pet,
Smiles now chasing frowns away
  From the face of Margaret.

Winsome little lass, may thou,
  Guileless in thy glee and fun,
Ne'er to Sorrow's mandate bow,
  Nor walk thorny paths upon.
Roses blooming at thy feet,
  With the dew of heaven wet,
Are to me not half so sweet
  As my little Margaret.

Oh, Thou, who dost guard and guide
  Little ones through sun and shade,
Keep her ever at Thy side ;
  Let her hand in Thine be laid !
May the sunshine she imparts
  Ne'er be dimmed by a regret ;
Loved is she by many hearts ;
  Little fair haired Margaret.

FREE CURRENCY.

Do not quarrel ; do not fret ;
Not the thing to do, you bet ;
Better take a sight of chaff,
Pass it by with quiet laugh,
Than work yourself into a pet
And be caught in passion's net !

Do not quarrel ; do not scold —
Smiles are silver ; laughs are gold !
What a grand world this would be
With such a free currency !
Better smile with eyelids wet,
Than fall into passion's net !

Do not quarrel nor complain —
Life's made up of sun and rain ;
Touch a life with rain or snow —
How the sweet heart-flowers grow !
There's peace for those who do not get
Tangled up in passion's net.

Do not murmur or repine ;
Hope ! 'Tis like a rare old wine !
Hope ! There's plenty and to spare ;
Hope ! 'Tis rising everywhere !
Better, though, its star should set,
Than fall into passion's net !

"Ring out, ye bells, on Christmas Day."

CHRISTMAS BELLS.

Ring out, ye bells, on Christmas Day,
  In happy, joyous strain ;
Let all the world with them rejoice,
  For the day has come again,
When to a waiting world there came,
  The long looked, wished for birth
Of One who came of low estate,
  To bless the expectant earth.

Bring holly berries, crimson red,
  Pine, fir and mistletoe,
Let all the children's hearts rejoice,
  For in the Golden Long Ago,
He was born, the Wonderful,
  Counselor, on earth to dwell,
Walking Judean streets about,
  God with us — Emanuel.

I've gazed upon the starry host,
  And wondered which the star
God honored thus, to be the guide
  Of Wise Men from afar.
How bright it must have shone that night,
  Conscious that its moving ray,
Would lead the seekers to the place
  Where the infant Jesus lay !

And then its work was just half done,
  For now, on Bethlehem's plain,
The shepherds saw a wondrous sight,
  And heard the grand refrain :
" Peace on Earth, good will to men : "
  Sung by the Angel Choir,
While all the sky was now ablaze
  With bright, celestial fire.

" Fear not ; for unto you is born,"
  The lingering angel said,
" Christ, the Lord, in Bethlehem,
  And in a manger laid ! "
Then lo ! the star to them appeared
  At once, with cheering ray.
And stood above the stable, where
  The sleeping Savior lay.

Oh, Earth, bring forth thy frankincense,
  Thy myrrh, thy hoarded gold.
Thy adoration for this King,
  Whose coming was foretold !
Not all the wealth that thou canst bring,
  Nor treasures yet to be,
Can equal in Love's balances,
  The love He has for thee !

The star, and what became of it,
  Your wond'ring hearts would ask ?
Perhaps God sent it to its place,
  Having fulfilled its task.

May be, in His great love for us,
  He caused it to grow dim,
That we might look beyond the star.
  And worship only Him !

Oh, glorious star ! Oh, glorious thread
  Which binds us all in love !
Never before, such Christmas Gift
  From loving hands above ;
So may our hearts be full of joy,
  With music, gifts and mirth,
Rejoicing in this day of days
  Blessed by a Savior's birth.

YOU KNOW IT.

To smile is better than to frown,
For smoothing ruffled feelings down,
      You know it !
Then why lament at every ill?
Is not the old world rolling still,
And sunshine kissing every hill?
      You know it !

Men can't redeem the minutes past,
Nor lift the shadows on them cast ;
      You know it !
But on life's road of weariness,
As footsore, tired pilgrims press,
A warm hand-clasp will often bless ;
      You know it !

Ambitions never reach their goal ;
Nor fill the hunger of the soul ;
      You know it !
I knew a king a conqueror, too.
Who sat and cried with loud boo-hoo,
Not having further work to do !
      You know it !

Man never reached the highest shelf,
By living solely for himself;
          You know it!
King Solomon, with all his pride
Of wealth, and many wives beside,
Confessed he was not satisfied!
          You know it!

One day a herald will appear,
And leave a message all must hear;
          You know it!
Then, very softly, one will tread,
Where lowly, lowly lies your head,
And say, " He loved me! He is dead! "
          You know it!

MISAPPREHENSION.

He read the book with great surprise
   And said, " How she abused her eyes!
She threw them at the frescoed ceiling;
   They fell as if they had no feeling;
Then rested them on the cool lagoon,
   And brought them back, ah, none too soon;
For with a cry and glad embrace,
   They fastened on her lover's face! "

A THANKSGIVING SUGGESTION.

The parson had preached from the beautiful text.
" Little children, love one another ; "
And he told of the mansions now being prepared
  By Jesus, the elder brother.
And he spoke of the River of Life, bright and clear.
  And the songs the redeemed will sing ;
And the palms they will wave and the crowns they will cast
  At the feet of Jesus, the King.

And oh, best of all, the friends we have loved
  Not lost but just gone before.
Who are waiting to greet us with fondest embrace.
  When we reach that evergreen shore ;
Where arms will be twined in a loving embrace
  Round the dear ones we've loved in this life ;
Where children as brothers and sisters will stand,
  With united husband and wife.

And he spoke of the love which Jesus imparts
  That he smiles from his bright home on high.
When we show to each other the love which he showed
  For a lost world to suffer and die.
" Oh, that wonderful love ! " the good parson said,
  " If you have it, my sister, my brother,
Let it flow in good works ; for as Christ has loved you,
  So ought ye to love one another ! "

Now Widower Gripem had lingered behind ;
" Oh, parson," he said, " tell me where
That beautiful place is. I long much to know,
    For I feel 'twould be sweet to be there ! "
" Next Thursday's Thanksgiving," the good parson said,
" Now there is our poor Widow Gray ;
Her larder is empty ; her hearthstone is cold —
    She should have a good dinner that day."

" Send up coal and potatoes, with flour and rice ;
    A turkey for roasting — and tea,
Cranberries for sauce, sugar-plums for the boys —
    And oh, how happy they'll be !
And then in the evening be sure that you go
    For with propriety surely you may—
And read one of David's most comforting psalms,
    Then kneel with the family and pray."

The advice was well taken   and oh, such a prayer,
    And oh, such a vision of bliss !
For peace, like a river, stole into his soul—
    And the widow's hand stole into his !
When robins were singing — as you may have guessed,
    In the spring time, when the weather was bright,
A wedding fee fell to the good parson's share —
    Now, pray, don't you think he was right ?

LOVELY MAY.

She stands in Summer's gateway,
  Lovely May,
With apron full of blossoms,
  Bright and gay :
Bringing showers, bright spring flowers,
Birds singing in green bowers,
Making sweet the passing hours,
  Every day.

Earth is brighter for thy coming,
  Gentle May ;
Our hearts lighter, faces brighter,
  For thy stay ,
For thou wilt our hearts prepare
For thy sister's coming, rare
June, with rose-garlanded hair,
  On the way !

THE FLOOD. 1892.

Oh, month of buds and roses,
  Of love and many flowers,
When Iowa, her bridal robes
  Puts, 'mid sun and showers.
She greets you with her moistened eye
  Believing that there still is
Some chances yet for growing crops,
  As well as water lilies !

THE SUNDAY SCHOOL'S FAREWELL.

Read at the Farewell Banquet, given by the Central Presbyterian Church and congregation of Des Moines, to Dr. and Mrs. Howard Agnew Johnston, November 16, 1893.

We all know just how hard it is to say the word " Good Bye ; "
And " Farewell," softly spoken, brings the moisture to the eye ;
Often, a close hand-clasp, while the head is turned away,
Will express the feelings better than any word that one could say.

Speech may sometimes be silver, when the heart is light and free.
But to-night the golden silence would be better still for me ;
But, as you have insisted on a speech from me in rhyme,
My coinage will be very free and silvery in its chime.

" The Sunday School." That is the theme I am to talk about :
" Our Sunday School." Dear friends, I think, without a doubt,
You know that in this glorious work for years I've borne a part,
And it's easy, quite, to speak of things that lie close to one's
     heart.

I sometimes let my memory travel back to '55,
To the ancient church on Fourth street — a busy little hive ;
Where teachers taught the children, and proved by earnest tones,
That the hive was full of working bees, with few, if any drones.

Whene'er I think of those old times my heart is strangely stirred,
And I always take my hat off when I think of Father Bird,
And his companion in the good work, his true and loving wife,
Who still holds up the banner he fought under all his life.

And what do Presbyterians owe such women and such men,
For our lamp, now burning brightly, which flickered feebly then?
Oh, answer it, my people, upon the bended knee,
That our lamp may burn so brightly, that all the world may see!

Our Sunday School. How large 'tis grown! It makes me ancient
        seem,
As I look at its beginnings. It's almost like a dream,
To see the girls and boys, who have sat upon my knees,
Wearing their gold-bowed spectacles and sporting families!

And speaking of our girls and boys of marriageable ages,
Why not let the old historian record upon his pages
That you'll follow their example, while there yet is room,
And give your Pastor, ere he goes, a matrimonial boom?

It does not seem to be the thing to cheat him of his fee,
Leaving his wife to vainly ask, " What shall the harvest be? "
I am inclined to blame the boys, for such a state of things;
For lack of courage, or, mayhap, a lack of wedding rings!

For our girls are so well grounded in the Scriptures that they can
Give an answer very promptly to every asking man!
Our Sunday School is sorry — but there's sweetness in the cup,
At the thought of how our preacher will stir Chicago up;

For after searching all the country, this big church had to join
In the calling of a pastor from the city of Des Moines.
We bow to fate most gracefully and think it for the best,
That Chicago should pay homage to talent farther west.

We will miss him in the songs we've sung, in which he bore a
    part ;
But he'll never get so far away but they'll echo in his heart.
We will not say farewell just now, but sing the sweet refrain,
" God be with you, God be with you, until we meet again."

PRECAUTION.

" My dear," he said in gentle tones,
    " I cannot, as expected,
Buy for you the seal skin sacque
    Which you have just selected.
You see I'm getting on in years,
    And say it with a sigh,
That old men are, as Solomon said,
    Afraid of all things high ! "

THE KICKER'S FUNERAL.

A kicker was kicking his very last kick
  For he'd kicked, (it was one of his ways,)
At his friends, at his neighbors, his fate and his town,
  And thus, finally ended his days.

It was not his sudden departure at all,
  That saddened everyone's face :
But as they remembered his acts while on earth,
  Felt sorry for " 'tother place ! "

So they buried him out in the wild, wild woods,
  In a deep, deep hole in the ground,
Where the straddle-bug straddled, and the grasshopper hopped,
  And the tumble-bug walked over his mound.

But some friends who admired his ways in this life,
  In numbers then gathered around,
To descant on his virtues and moisten with tears
  Of sorrow, the newly made mound.

When remarks were in order, a wiggle-worm came,
  And said, as he wiggled about
" This brother of mine, when a tight place was found,
  Always wiggled so carefully out ! "

A raven which listened with countenance grave,
   As he sat on the limb of an oak,
With awe-stricken voice said, " I part with regret,
   With him who first taught me to croak ! "

A sorrowing mule then discoursed to the crowd : —
" My friends, it makes me quite sick,
To part with this brother and teacher as well ;
   For 'twas he who first taught me to kick ! "

A hog which was rooting a little way off,
   Came forward and said with deep feeling :
" For the first time in life I am mourning for one
   Who surpassed me in grunting and squealing ! "

A crawfish came cautiously out of his hole,
   And exclaimed after some reflection
" Alas my brother ! For years and for years,
   We've progressed in the same direction ! "

These eloquent speakers then glided away.
   Having spoken their pieces like sages ;
And the " Kicker," if he is not asked for a cent,
   Will slumber in peace there for ages !

RETURN OF THE PRODIGALS.

We've jest got back to Iowa   tell you, we've had it rough ;
Of hunting up new countries, we've had jest about enough ;
You bet, me and Mirandy is a pretty seedy lot,
But it's good sometimes to thank the Lord fer what ye hav'n't
    got !   .

We kinder got dissatisfied with Iowa years ago ;
Mirandy's lungs were powerful weak to stand the wind and snow ;
An' while we was a thinkin' there came along that drought,
While Mirandy kept a coughin' and a talkin' 'bout the south.

We'd heerd that Kansas wus the land where milk and honey
    flowed
So free, that we could dip it up. fer anything we knowed ;
With land jest fer the askin', and climit throwed in free
Mirandy cleared her throat and said. " That's jest the place fer
    me ! "

So we moved down into Kansas, in eighteen eighty-eight,
And built a little sod house and settled down to wait
Till our corn was in the roastin' ear. There came with hummin'
    sound,
An army of grasshoppers   an' they et to the ground !

' She coughed a penitential cough an' whispered — ' Iowa!' "

"So we moved down into Kansas."

Next year we planted corn agin. Tell yer, upon my word,
A hot wind swept the State and left our crop like Jonah's gourd
Withered in a single night! Tell ye, we had the blues,
And wondered what Miranda's pap would say about the news.

He'd wanted us to come back home, and said, without a doubt
He could feed us cheaper there, than by sendin' projuce out;
While we was a hesitatin' 'bout what we'd better do,
We had a revelation which thrilled us through and through.

We went to preachin' meetin' 'bout fourteen miles away
An' I'll not forget that sermon up to my dyin' day;
The preacher told about a boy who left his father's roof
With all his goods and chattels, for his own use and behoof.

Goin' west to speckerlate he soon became dead broke;
Then friends, like cash or bonds and sich, all vanished like the
          smoke;
He "took a tumble to himself," after he'd had a cry,
And said, "My father's hired men have better grub than I!"

So home went, in want and rags he could not well conceal
Had royal welcome, interspersed with fiddlin' and veal !
The preacher paused a minit then, with voice uplifted high,
Said, " Return, ye prodigals, return, for wherefore will you die,

By eatin' husks, that don't digest, and wearin' rags of sin ? "
My eyes were over-brimmin' an' my head begin to spin ;
I turned 'round to Mirandy, to see what she would say ;
She coughed a penitential cough, an' whispered " Iowa ! "

  * * * * * *

Her pap sent on some money, an' she sold her weddin' ring,
An' we jest lit out fer Iowa, where corn is allus king !
Mirandy's cough ? You think it's strange, and, curious, perhaps —
She hasn't barked a single time, sence gittin' back to pap's.

Change of climit ? I guess not I rayther am inclined
To think that 'stid of climit, she has a change of mind !
We left our " good bye " on the walls of the house we couldn't
  sell
" No coal, no wood, no water and jest a half a mile from
  h l ! "

AMERICA'S CROWN.

Let the rose bloom for Old England,
  Shamrock for Ireland grow.
For Scotland her bold thistle,
  France, the lily, white as snow ;
But as for proud America,
  Where Plenty fills the horn,
And pours out an unending stream,
  Crown her with Golden Corn !
In hopes of coming years to see
  Her crownings will far richer be !

TO A NOVEMBER DANDELION.

NOTE.—Tacitus Hussey, the poet, was met on the street yesterday, wearing in his button-hole a beautiful dandelion. This flower was picked in the high school yard yesterday, a most peculiar time of the year for such a growth. A poem on the rare occurrence may be expected. Iowa State Register, November 16, 1891.

And dost thou bloom, dear little flower of May,
   When the swift-winged bird, glad, southward flies,
When bees have left the clover; when the day
   Is veiled in smoke, and cold the Autumn skies?
How sweet of thee, dear star-faced Taraxacum,
   To dare the dangers of the snow and frost;
Braving the season of the Chrysanthemum,
   And show thy smiling face at any cost!

Dear, bright dandelion! Thy name, whoever gave,
   Unrolls thy character to us as written scroll;
" Dandy " suggests thy rich attire, and " lion," brave;
   So, " Dandelion," one sweet, euphonious whole.
Dear waif! Knowest thou not that flower and bird
   Have flown and died, by wise laws of Nature fixed?
Soundless the woods   nor " cuckoo's " note is heard,
   Since the great " snow storm " of November sixth!

Untimely bloom ! I take thee to my heart
  In love, remembering happier scenes ;
A hungering world supposes it the part
  Of dandelions to bloom in spring — " for greens ! "
Oh, bride of May, with hoar frost for thy bed !
  Engraven on our hearts, thy lessons given :
In weather cold or hot, may it be said,
  We did our best as in the sight of heaven !

A SURPRISE.

I sought for Pleasure far and wide ;
  " Oh, Happiness ! " I said :
" Come share my lot ; be thou my bride,
    And let us quickly wed ! "
  Just then stern Duty caught my eye,
    And drew me to her side
  And said : " Fair Pleasure soon will die,
    But I will e'er abide."
  Then I wed Duty—and eftsoons I saw
    That I had Pleasure for a mother-in-law !

MEMORY'S SONG.

On the banks of the Wabash, so bright, I was born,
In a cabin of logs, 'mid pumpkins and corn,
My heart turns back as my birthplace I view,
For I love her grand forests and people don't you?

CHORUS.
Then sing, Hoosiers, sing, with hearts glad and free,
For with each rolling year she seems dearer to me.

With hearts full of good cheer, we've gathered to-day,
To exchange our kind greetings and in gratitude lay
A wreath of affection and love, twined about,
For the State that has sent so many good people out.

We love thy old forests, dear State of our birth,
The tallest and thickest of any on earth ;
Thy hills and thy valleys, and rivers so clear,
And all thy old memories we'll ever hold dear.

If you take bright sea shell from its home on the lea,
Wherever it goes it will sing of the sea ;
So we, like the sea shells, thus greet you to-day,
And sing for our old home, forever and aye.

HOOSIER ECHOES.

I reckon I have heard, durin' my long term of life,
    Most all the music nature has in store.
From a Whippo'rwill's lamentin' to a brass band's noisy strife,
    The Guinea hen and cyclone's fearful roar.
It is only when my mem'ry goes a calahootin' back
    To the Indianny forests, grand and free,
That there's jest one missin' card from out of mem'ry's pack —
    The hog call, " Pig-o-o-e-e. Pig-o-o-e-e. Pig-o-o-e-e ! "

My ! How a feller's mem'ry gits back to them old days,
    When the woods were all aglow with Nature's tints,
On the crisp an' frosty mornin's, when the mists began to raise,
    An' the coolin' winds of autumn gave us hints
That old winter was a comin' ; but near a big corn pile,
    Stood an artist, with a voice like soundin' sea,
Who woke the mornin' echoes, and all sleepers for a mile,
    With his loud " Pig-o-o-e-e, Pig-o-o-e-e, Pig-o-o-e-e ! "

Then, mebbe, 'cross the clearin', would come the ringin' sound,
    Which trembled on the circumambient air,
Where a neighbor was a callin' to all the country round,
    An' announcin' to his hogs that he was there !

Then, one by one, his neighbors took up the glad refrain
  In chorus grand, it allus seemed to me :
An' with full inflated lungs, they echoed back again,
  The well-known cry, " Pig-o-o-e-e, Pig-o-o-e-e, Pig-o-o-e-e ! "

An' the hogs ! You'd oughter seen 'em, as with one accord they
    broke
  For the feedin' places, gruntin' as they ran,
A crowdin', an' a pushin', an' a squealin' like some folk
  Who sometimes lead the office-seekin' van !
They're music-lovin' critters, them Indianny swine,
  An' hog callers there are allus in demand :
Their voices are their fortunes, an' they are artists in their line,
  For 'tis music, ears an' stomach, understand.

When the sun, through haze and smoke, blotted out the mornin'
    stars,
  From log cabin, mayhap, stepped a maiden fair,
With milkpail on her arm, trippin' to the pastur' bars,
  While the mornin' breeze toyed idly with her hair :
An' to the " pig-o-o-e-e " cry she'd add her treble notes,
  (While the meek-eyed cows their heads expectant toss :)
With melody as sweet as e'er came from robins' throats,
  She'd carol forth, " Sook-boss, Sook-boss, Sook-boss ! "
.

There's professors in our schools, who read Latin books all day,
  And talk in Greek to students at their work,
Who could not call " pig-o-o-e-e " in an enticin' way
  Ef their families was a sufferin' fer pork !
An' there's graduatin' women all over our Hawkeye State.

Whose education caused their parents loss.
Who speak of cows as " wild-eyed critters," and, oh, sad to relate,
  Know nothing of the music of " Sook-boss ! "

I git so tarnal tired of brass bands, an' soundin' bells,
  Piano jinglin's, mandolins and sich,
That I long for quiet rest in Nature's wooded dells, —
  Or a mountain top — I'm not a carin' which !
There comes to me in dreams - leastwise, when I can sleep
  Sound of bells of purest silver, purged of dross ;
An' it allus takes the form, in its sweet, resistless sweep,
  Of the musical " pig-o-o-e-e " and " sook-boss ! "

RISING GENIUS.

  A habit, Ebenezer had,
    Of sleeping late of mornings ;
  And this he'd do in spite of fate,
    And many wifely warnings.
  She gave him yeast cakes well disguised.
    As that idea seemed to seize her,
  And had no trouble after that
    To " raise her Ebenezer ! "

JUBILEE YEAR.

Well, this is "jub'lee year" for sure   see how they're coming
    back
To Iowa, the garden spot, where there's never any lack
Of food for every hungry man   no questioning 'bout creed
Our Iowa stands with hands outstretched to give to all who need.

And "Party Prodigals" there are, who, catching the refrain
Of harmony in the G. O. P., are flocking back again ;
The funniest thing about it all, is, without a doubt,
The honest look they all put on, when they say, "we've not been
    out !"

There was onc't a drunken fellow riding on a coach's top :
It gave a lurch, he lost his head and took another drop ;
Rising with drunken dignity said, with 'pologetic cough :
"I 'sposed the darned old thing upset   er I wouldn'ter got off !"

The old "wheel horses" coming back and hitching to the cart,
Are hints to us, the younger ones, that we must do our part ;
You bet that we will do it, too, remembering well that they,
In years gone by, have "borne the heat and burden of the day !"

I'm sure it is not very strange, when our stomachs get askew,
That we see all objects through a glass, deeply and densely blue !
Our livers get to "cutting up," and thus our brain befogs,
And say our country's "going to the everlasting dogs !"

And then again, we all get tired of everlasting grind ;
Doing just as the deacon did, which I have in mind -
His preacher found him " biling drunk," and asked, " Why, what
    is this ? "
Said the deacon with asperity, " I'll tell you how it is —

" I've served the Lord for forty years, without a cent of pay.
And I kinder calculated that I've earned a holiday ! "
Well, maybe that's the way with us but now we've " had our
    whirl,"
We'll step into the ranks again our banners to unfurl ;

For now you see we're satisfied and willing to return,
And join you in the conflict, " while the lamp holds out to
    burn ! "
For here of office provender there is a fearful lack,
And like the wife of Lot we've been for sometime " looking
    back ! "

With " Old Glory " floating o'er us, which made the rebels flee,
And marked Bold Sherman's pathway from Atlanta to the sea-
Victory will crown our flag, and you bet we will be there,
To make a modest mention that " Me and Betsey killed the
    Bear ! "

A SPRING BEAUTY.

Hey, little lily girl !
Has mamma turned you out to grass,
Where breezes fan you as they pass,
And sun can kiss you, little lass?
    Hey, little lily girl !

Hey, little lily girl !
Were I the sun, I'd kiss your head,
And tint your cheeks with dainty red,
And paint your lips like scarlet thread ;
    Hey, little lily girl !

Hey, little lily girl !
Were I the breeze, with fingers bold,
I'd tangle up your locks of gold,
And hear your mamma gently scold ;
    Hey, little lily girl !

Hey, little lily girl !
Were I the smiling, distant skies,
I'd come to earth, with glad surprise,
To borrow azure from your eyes ;
    Hey, little lily girl !

Hey, little lily girl !
If you were mine, how would I pray,
To feel your hand clasps every day,
Lest, on bright wings, you'd fly away ;
    Hey, little lily girl !

"Hey, Little Lily Girl!"

THE GOOD OLD TIMES.

I reckon we're agoin' to hev them good old times agin,
An' git back to furst principles. So I hev kinder bin
A polishin' up my mem'ry, and a gittin' my sails set,
So's me an' Mirandy kin sail on, without a gittin' wet.

There comes a lot of mem'rys, a crowdin' up by score,
A standin' just like soldiers, in ranks before yer door,
As you set there, with pipe alight — you want to ast 'em in
The hull blamed kit an' bilin' an' keep 'em ef you kin.

I like to think of good old times, 'bout fifty years ago,
When I wore blue jeans, for service, an' didn't keer fer show,
Ner frip'rees, sech as we hev now — ner walk in fashion's way —
Cuttin' Indianny cord wood at fifty cents a day,

An' take yer pay in bacon — or, maybe, good corn meal —
Walkin' homeward, in the gloamin', how good it made you feel ;
With good corn bread an' bacon — or " rye an' injun' " mixed —
You could jest knock hunger end ways, if that was how you're
    fixed.

The " dollar of our daddies " was skeerce in them ere days,
An' when we used to git one, 'twas one of our sly ways
To hide it in the shuck bed, er put underneath
The hearthstone, to keep it handy fer cuttin' baby teeth,

Er lend it round the settlement, to some onlucky neighbor,
Who wrestled at all seasons, with very ill-paid labor—
Fer in them days of simple livin', it didn't allus foller,
That the man with best filled quiver, allus had the silver dollar.

Farm projuce was uncommon low, and store goods awful high,
'Bout fifty cents fer calico, er common factory.
An' eggs, three cents a dozen, an' even, maybe, then,
You'd find that you'd been underlaid, by a more industrious hen.

There was no tax on luxuries, in them days, of any sort,
You could buy yer whisky by the bar'l, at 'bout ten cents a
    quart :
There was no chance of sellin' yer corn, wheat, rye or beans,
'Less you loaded 'em on flat-boats, an' tuck 'em down to New
    Orleans.

Bin thinkin' 'bout a bran' new house, me and Mirandy had,
The clapboard roof was leakin' some, an' the chimbly kinder bad,
The daubin' had a fallen out with the chinkin' an' got loose,
So we thought the new one was in sight and repairin' want much
    use ;

But when the 'lection news came in, I kinder changed my plan,
I'll patch it up an' then turn in, an' do the best I can ;
I told my joy an' sorrow partner just what we'd hev to do
An' Mirandy sed, an' sed it loud, " Boo-hoo, boo-hoo, boo-hoo ! "

I'll chink and daub it all around, to keep free trade wind out,
An' corn shucks in the floor cracks will be protection, I've no
    doubt ;
For me, the future haint got no bright anticipations,
'Less the People's party "gets there," an' issues gov'ment rations.

Old Podunk says it come about, by livin' up too high;
Naber Stebbins says he thinks it come from reciprocity;
I swan, I don't know what to think, but feel kind o' suspicious,
It come about by people bein' " onnaterally wicious."

EASTER MORNING.

We hail thee, joyous Easter Day,
  While drowsy Earth, in happiness,
Opes timid eyes from winter's sleep,
And from low plain and rocky steep
  Make haste to don her vernal dress,
While robins sing a roundelay.

Oh, Easter Day, upon the breath
  Of early spring comes this grand thought;
That He who slept in rocky tomb,
'Mid hours of deep encircling gloom,
  Has mankind's resurrection wrought,
By breaking prison bars of death.

CHRISTMAS.

You can tell of coming Christmas,
 By the jingling of the bells,
By the many happy faces,
Which are blooming in all places,
 Where the busy merchant sells.
By the Christmas trees on sidewalk,
 By the turkeys, big and fat ;
By well-behaving girls and boys,
Expectant of new Christmas joys,
 Remembering " where they're at ! "

By the many merry greetings,
 By the softened hearts of all ;
By the patient time abiding,
And the very careful hiding
 Of presents, great and small.
And so our thoughts are turning
 To the sweetest of all days,
When Love goes out a smiling,
Her lap with presents piling,
 Singing songs of joy and praise !

THE POET'S PLEA.

" Singer, where do you find your joyous songs? "
   I find them always ready made for me ;
There's scarce an object in this world of ours,
   But can be turned to sweetest poesy.
The great wheel at the busy factory hums
   A melody to my untutored ears,
Much sweeter than the grandest, swelling song
   E'er set to music by the rolling spheres.

The joyous notes of happy, whistling men,
   Who, freed from labor's carking, weary grind,
Whistling, homeward trudge, loved ones to greet,
   Is best and grandest music to my mind.
My fancy pictures, where, in humble homes,
   The fires of love upon the altars burn.
The wife's bright smile, the prattling children's kiss,
   To welcome the tired father's glad return.

The noxious thistle, with its winged seeds,
   Is full to overflowing with reflection's food
To thoughtful men. Teaching us tnat we may sow,
   Unwittingly, the seeds of bad and good.

How sweet 'twill be, if, at the end of days,
  When life's sun dips beneath the summer sea,
To think, God willing, that our good seed sown,
  May find rich soil in nations yet to be !

The organ grinder, on our public street,
  Or, as he serves me at my very door,
Reminds me oft that, better far his work,
  Than grinding e'er the faces of the poor !
Pathetic, too, it seems withal, to me :
  Trudging about with " weary step and slow "
He sadly points to me that time in life
  When all the sounds of grinding will be low.

The bird, which cleaves the air on tireless wing,
  Is a sweet poem, ever dear to me :
For, without chart or compass, lo ! its flight
  Is guided over unknown lands and sea.
Then, will not He, who gave me, unasked, life,
  And placed my feet upon the thorny road,
Well marked by stones, all stained by bleeding feet,
  Bring me at last, to His own blest abode ?

The chrysalis, with hidden germ enclosed,
  Has naught pleasing to unobservant eyes :
And yet, with patient waiting, warmth and care,
  Comes forth the gauzy, bright-winged butterflies.
Will not He, who holds worlds in boundless space,
  Whose care extends to groveling things of earth,
Give us such form as seemeth good to Him,
  When haply, we receive our second birth ?

And ask you, then, where do I find my songs?
    They come to me in country or in town ;
The wind, the sun, the rivers whisper me,
    And I? I only gladly write them down.
'Tis easy when you know just what to say :
    The field is large and pleasant is the work
If you have praise, bestow it on the Muse,
    For I am just her confidential clerk !

SPRING.

She is coming up the valley,
    She is climbing o'er the hills,
Strewing flowers to the music
    And the laughter of the rills.
With Violets and Spring Beauties
    Her dainty hands she fills.

She is coming up the valley,
    Bringing with her lengthened days,
Keeping time to merry song birds
    And inspiring matin lays,
Mingling spring time's welcome music
    With children's out door plays.

GOIN' TO FARMIN'.

Goin' to farm, me and Miranda is ;
    That's what President Stickney says ;
" Crappin' it," now is jest the biz,
    So President Stickney says.
Sez he, " The cities haint got room ;
Ef ye want to escape the impendin' doom,
Git out or starve in one small room ! "
    So President Stickney says.

Now, out door life is jest the chalk.
    That's what President Stickney says ;
So 'bout five millions hev got to walk,
    So President Stickney says,
Out on the land and raise big " craps,"
To feed the ling'ring suburban chaps,
And we'll all be happier perhaps ;
    So President Stickney says.

" What people want is more to eat ! "
    That's what President Stickney says,
" For big crops, Iowa's hard to beat ! "
    So President Stickney says.

" So we're goin' to do our level best,
  To feed the hungry an' oppressed
  Fillin' vacuums of those distressed ! "
    That's what Mirandy says.

" All wealth must be dug from the ground ! "
      That's what President Stickney says,
  So folks had better look around,
      So President Stickney says,
  For a place to dig. And then begin
  To dig like everlastin' sin,
  To git cities on their feet agin !
      So President Stickney says.

" Now, farmin' haint so all fired hard ! "
      That's what President Stickney says ;
  Sez he, " I'm speakin' by the card ! "
      So President Stickney says.
" Makes difference though, jest where you ar',
  Er view it, from anear or far - -
  From hay rack or a palace car ! "
      That's what Mirandy says.

" Yov're wantin' prosperous times agin ! "
      That's what President Stickney says ;
" Git out on the farms and fetch her in ! "
      So President Stickney says.
" We haint the kind as'll stand aroun'
  And see our gov'ment go down,
  Jest 'cause we want to live in town ! "
      That's what Mirandy says.

Five millions of us hev got to go !
   That's what President Stickney says.
To ease the cities' overflow :
   So President Stickney says.
" Say ! Got a good farm anywheres ?
We'll leave the city and its snares,
And " go to crappin' on the shares ! "
   That's what Mirandy says.

TEARS MINGLED.

She lost her ear-rings in the well :
   Alas, and a-lack-a day !
She wept and mourned about it,
   Till her lover came that way.

Why did he mingle tears with hers,
   Nor words of chiding spoke ?
He remembered when he bought them,
   How he put his watch " in soak ! "

COLUMBUS DAY.

We're goin' to hist the good old flag, me and my wife, Mirandy,
Been lookin' for'ard to the day, and kept " Old Glory " handy :
So, when Columbus day arrives, no matter what the weather,
We'll fly it from the roof, and shout for Christopher together.

You bet it makes old folks feel good, and sets the blood a bilin',
To think about Ameriky and her flag with stars a smilin' ;
An' all the way we hev bin led by Him who has delivered
Our country from her perils oft, sence we hev bin diskivered.

Ef it hadn't been for Christopher's inquirin' disposition,
A long felt want an' cravin' heart to better his condition,
What would we all hev bin to-day ? History supposes
We'd be eatin' acorns round a fire with brass rings in our noses !

An' a wearin' 'coon an' 'possum skins, a livin on half rations,
An' a dancin' them ghost dances like the other Indian nations !
We'd ort to thank Queen Isabel, fer the blessin's which surround
        us —
But fer her money's talkin', Chris never could hev found us.

Great many people in this land haint got no comprehension
'Bout the bigness of the enterprise that history makes mention ;
But jest set down and argy, and turn in and insist it
Was sech a big track of land he never could hev missed it !

Some folks say that he was stuck on hisself, as navigator
But I can't find sech facts confirmed by any old narrator
Don't b'lieve he cared a copper cent fer hist'ry's future pages,
But ter find a land to waltz round in 'thout fallin' off the
     aiges !

Well, I guess yes, he found it, too, this Capting of the Pinto ;
Though San Salvador was the fust place Columbus entered into
I've allus thought it was a shame, sence he was out a coastin'.
To stop at sech a one-hoss place when he could hev sailed to
     Bostin,

An' made them Bostin folks feel good, an' gay as a red wagon.
By addin' to their stock in trade of things they like to brag on ;
May be, though, it's jest as well ter those days of hist'ry dim,
As they might now all be claimin' that they diskivered him !

Many a man in these fast times would hev fretted at delay,
While Isabel was gettin' ships ter him to sail away ;
Columbus sweetly smiled at fate an' didn't get disgusted
An' he wa'n't afeerd of collary, et his pictures kin be trusted !

My eyes git kinder misty like, thinkin' of Columbia's lack
In them tryin' days, she didn't hev a hull flag to her back
But now, from drizzly Oregon to Maine's high rocky shore,
She's dressed in stars an', woman-like, is hollerin' fer more !

So me an' Mirandy, we will fly the starry flag together ;
We'll hist it from our cabin roof in any sort of weather ;
We don't keer fer rain that wets, er a cold wave that benumbs
     us,
We'll jest turn in an' shout our best fer Christopher Columbus.

Our Iowa, among other lands, was diskivered somewhat later,
By men who've made her what she is. Kin you pint out a
 greater ?
Up with " Old Glory " then, that day ! Put the flag-staff in the
 socket
There's no persimmon up so high but Iowa's pole kin knock it !

THE TARIFF.

She was so tall and he so short,
 She said 'twere only fair,
If he really wished to kiss her,
 He must stand up on a chair ;
Then climbing down, in raptures,
 He said : " Look a here, Mariar ;
That's a splendid illustration
 Of sugar getting higher ! "

CHRISTMAS CAROL.

Christmas songs are in the air,
    Caroling sweet :
Answering voices everywhere,
    The strains repeat.
Love and Peace walk hand in hand,
    Whispering low ;
Scattering blessings o'er the land,
    They singing go.

Christmas songs are in the air,
    Echoing wide ;
Tossed by voices here and there,
    At Christmas tide.

Hope and Joy, with arms entwined,
    Wandering forth,
Touch the hearts of all mankind,
    O'er all the earth.

Christmas songs are in the air :
    The angels' song,
Sung to wond'ring shepherds there,
    Their sheep among,
Is echoing 'round the circling earth,
    And blessing them,
Who sing the song of the glad birth,
    At Bethlehem !

Christmas songs are in the air,
    Oh, human heart !
With sweetest music everywhere,
    Wilt bear a part,
To swell the joyous Christmas song,
    With voice of praise,
And thus with melody prolong,
    This day of days !

WOULD LIKE ANOTHER CHANCE.

These times are not what they used to be, I hear the old men
    say ·
In school modes, or in colleges, in business, work or play ;
The folks who got their schooling in the days so long gone by,
Look with envy on the present ways, and draw a weary sigh.
The trouble is, as I suspect, our early date of birth,
Ere Knowledge, with her nimble feet, ran swiftly o'er the earth ;
And Wisdom cried about the streets, her virtues to enhance
So, after all, I don't know but I'd like another chance !

I miss the old slab seats and the fireplace long and wide ;
The high and slanting writing desks, along the rough logs' side ;
I miss the squeaky quill pens, with home-made ink made wet,
As in falt'ring hands they followed the copy that was set
" Command you may, your minds from play   " 'twas pretty
    hard to do
In those old days, I wonder if 'tis easier in the new ?
I hope the rule of love, these days, all cruelty supplants,
Making the old log school house boys long for another chance !

I miss the good old-fashioned games we used to play at noon
That hour seemed the shortest   study coming all too soon ;
Ah, those dear old games of " Shinny," " Town Ball," and
    " Crack the Whip ; "

And the laugh we'd give the fellow, when he'd sometimes " loose
    his grip ! "
Your modern game of foot-ball has in it, many tumbles,
With " touchdowns," " tackles," " rushes," and many awkward
    " fumbles ; "
The requisites would seem to be, long hair and padded pants —
So I reckon old log school house boys don't care to take a
    chance !

I miss the old love letters, with the picture of two hearts,
Pierced, and held together, with most wonderful of darts,
With the oft-repeated statement :   " If you love me as I love
    you."
No knife, yet manufactured, " Can cut our love in two ! "
Ah, me ! How much of budding love, this sentiment enshrines ;
How many hearts have fluttered, with the reading of these lines !
Some say marriage is a lottery or else a short romance ;
But all the boys and girls I know, would like to take a chance !

Our bodies may grow old ; but hearts should ever be kept young —
Hang not your harps on willows, neglected and unstrung ;
But sing your songs of gladness, that all the world may hear —
Who can tell what ears are open to catch your notes of cheer ?
Some men, and very good ones, too, forget they once were boys,
And frown upon hilarity, or anything like noise ;
And shut their hearts 'gainst fiddles — and the chaste and merry
    dance —
But I " Swan to man ! " I don't know but I'd like another
    chance !

THE OLD RAIN BARREL.

Oh, the dripping of the water from the eaves,
  What music it has always been to me ;
'Neath cabin roof where rustling forest leaves
  Joined the dripping in the sweetest melody ;
      With the steady, ceaseless dripping.
      As' from clapboards it came tripping,
        To the music of the leaves ;
      Dropping, dropping, never stopping,
        In its drip, drip, dripping.
Into the old rain barrel, 'neath the eaves.

I've heard many fancy operas in my time ;
  Hand organs and pianos till I'm tired ;
Brass bands and sounding cymbals as they chime,
  With wealth of lungs and muscles well inspired ;
      But more soothing to my spirit,
      Is the water, when I hear it,
        As a song my memory weaves,
      Mingling with the rythmic dropping,
        Dripping, dripping, dropping,
Into the old rain barrel, 'neath the eaves !

Ah, 'mid the scenes of plenty how the heart
   Clings, vine-like, to the happy days of yore,
While floods of memories cause the tears to start,
   At the thought that such sounds may come no more,
      As the rippling, aqueous lapping,
      And the gentle, ceaseless tapping,
         The weary brain relieves :
      As it falls with rippling measure,
         Dripping, dripping, dropping.
Into the old rain barrel, 'neath the eaves.

The heart cry of the world is, " I'm a-weary ! "
   Looking forward to the sunset of our days,
How our souls murmur softly, " Miserere ! "
   As we plod slowly on our winding ways :
      But our memories never sleeping,
      E'er reminds us of the weeping,
         Of the eaves trough as it grieves,
      Weeping the sombre night away,
         With its drip, drip, dropping.
Into the old rain barrel, 'neath the eaves !

Weary, sleepless, turn I to the book of yore,
   While Hope turns with loving hands the leaves,
And she gives me the bright promise that once more,
   I may sleep to the sound of dropping eaves,
      Kissing down my eyelids sweetly,
      Shutting out the world completely —
         Nor mockingly deceives
      Weary ones who love the dripping,
         Dripping, dripping, dropping,
Of the rainfall in the barrel, 'neath the eaves !

PROSPERITY.

She is standing on the mountain top,
With eyes turned to the West
With thoughtful look and attitude she stands ;
Her footsteps west are tending,
Though her way seems never ending,
In its slowness   but she's mending
And her coming will set humming
All the idle wheels in Iowa's broad land !

Yes, she's coming through the valley,
With timid step and slow
How joyously we'll greet her when she comes !
With all sorts of floral missles,
And a thousand factory whistles
While the Wolf with rising bristles,
From workman's door retreats before
Prosperity's procession with her drums !

THE TEMPLE BEAUTIFUL.

We are building, we are building,
    My little wife and I,
A temple called " The Beautiful,"
    Nor lands do we possess;
The foundation is the Solid Rock,
    Its turrets reach the sky,
The pillars which support them
    Are Love and Faithfulness.

Its walls will be adorned with
    Many goodly stones,
Brought from the mines of Cheerfulness,
    And curiously wrought,
By years of weary toil, mayhap,
    And many tears and groans,
With which life's sad experience
    Is often dearly bought.

Our rooms will all be beautiful,
    With everything so grand;
Here Faith will fold her tired wings.
    And settle down to rest,

And Hope, upon a pretty little
    Pedestal will stand,
While Charity will have a place
    Where pleaseth her the best.

The process has been very slow,
    As, one by one, the stones
Have found the right position
    In the slowly rising wall :
And ah ! the sad mistakes we've made,
    Which memory bemoans,
And replacing the defective ones,
    In sadness we recall.

Oft times, when storm clouds lower,
    We'll climb the turrets high,
Hand clasped in hand with Faith and Hope,
    To view the farther shore
Of the land of Hope and Promise,
    Which sometimes seems so nigh,
As it lies in quiet grandeur,
    Our home for evermore.

Some day, not now, in other lands,
    We'll read with moistened eyes,
The meaning of our crosses here,
    And deep, unuttered sighs :
And kiss the hand we could not see,
    Because our eyes were dull,
For polishing these tear-washed stones,
    For " Temple Beautiful."

We are building, we are building,
   My little wife and I,
A temple called " The Beautiful."
   Nor lands have we possessed,
And oh ! the joy 'twill give us.
   If, in the bye and bye,
The temple is accepted by
   The King of Righteousness.

WHICH ?

The New Woman and the Old Man
   Discussed, the other day,
Deep and portentous questions ;
   And each one had a say.
But the discussion waxed the hottest.
   When they settled down to this
Momentous question, whether
   " Bloomers are ? " or " bloomers is ? "

A THANKSGIVING TOAST.

November, with Thanksgiving, passes out ;
  December, with its Christmas, cometh in ;
We say farewell to first, with feast and shout,
  Then prepare for the happy Christmas din.
And thus it is, the dear old earth goes round,
  Bringing gladness to so many girls and boys ;
But not to them alone, for I'll be bound,
  The old folks will be sharers in their joys.

In November, walk we 'mid the falling leaves,
  'Neath the sun's close-veiled and smoky glow ;
In December, where old Winter's tempest grieves,
  Sowing lavishly, the treasures of his snow.
And thus the fleeting seasons, one by one,
  Glide so quietly that they hardly leave a trace ;
For the summer season is no sooner done
  Than the sun kisses earth's averted face.

In November, heap we up, in golden piles,
  God's best gift to our Iowa   golden corn ;
December, greet we her with tears and smiles,
  For, in her death, the glad new year is born.
Thus the days, months and years, in cycles come,
  And their beauties to the eyes of all unveil,
Leaning on the promise, of which this is the sum :
  " Seed time and harvest shall not fail."

In November, lift we grateful eyes above,
  To Him, for the fruitage of the year ;
In December, give we feasts and gifts of love,
  Filling earth full of joyous, happy cheer.
And thus, in the changing future years,
  May each heart, with happiness, be crowned,
Looking up, oft through many smiles and tears,
  To the great Love, which makes the world go round.

THE ROUNDUP.

" What ? Old John Goldbug dead ? How sad !
    And didn't leave a cent ?
  Why, he was rich as Crœsus was
    I wonder where it went ! "
  And then the sorrowing heir replied :
  " You see he lost his health
  In getting rich. To get that back,
    He then lost all his wealth ! "

THE HOMESICK HOOSIER.

I've been thinkin', lately, thinkin' of my old home in Indianny,
   An' the cabin 'mid the beech wood, 'bout forty years gone
      past ;
An' I've tried to pictur' in my mind the many, many changes,
   Though I like to think her over jest as I saw her last.

I'd like so much again to hear the old cock pheasant " drummin' "
   In the thicket, on the old log, he used from day to day ;
That was his idee of courtin' but don't let him hear you comin'
   Er he'll slip down in the hazel bresh and hide hisself away.

En I want to go onct more to a good old-fashioned sugarin'
  En watch its granulations as the " stirrin' paddle " whirls
En when you talk of sweetness, I hev lost my reckolecshun
  As to jest how I decided ' 'twixt the sugar an' the girls !

En ef it wasn't wicked, I'd like to, jest onct more,
  Step off " Money Musk," or " Chase the Squirrel," upon a
    puncheon floor :

I never keerd fer waltzin' to the fiddle's witchin' sound
  You kin hug a gal much better when she haint a " bobbin
    'round ! "

An' I want to jest set down to a good, old-fashioned dinner ;
  Corn pone and biled pertaters, " chicken fixins " on the right,
Corn beef and cabbage, jowl an' greens, with artichokes an'
      onions ;
  Roast pig with apple sass, or jell   an' everything in sight.

Ef everything's before ye, ye can make some calkerlation,
  An' kinder map out in your mind jest what yer want to do ;
But when there's only dishes, ye kaint make prognostication
  Regardin' what you're goin' to hev   ontil ye most get through !

I never could get onto this new-fangled way of feedin',
  Fetchin' a little, timid like, as ef they thought 'twas pore ;
En when ye'd settled down on somethin' suited to your eatin',
  Whisk off the dishes, knives an' forks, an' fetch along some
      more ;

En settin' at the table, mebbe, 'bout three hours or over,
  En changin' dishes 'leven times, an' poppin' champaign corks

Ef I was mowin' hay away as bizzy as tarnation,
  Ye bet I wouldn't want to stop an be a changin' forks !

I kin count my herds of cattle by the thousand, on the hillside,
  Perarie land by sections, household treasures money couldn't
    buy -
But ef I had the calm content of that cabin in the beech wood
  I wouldn't swap it off — not for mansions in the sky !

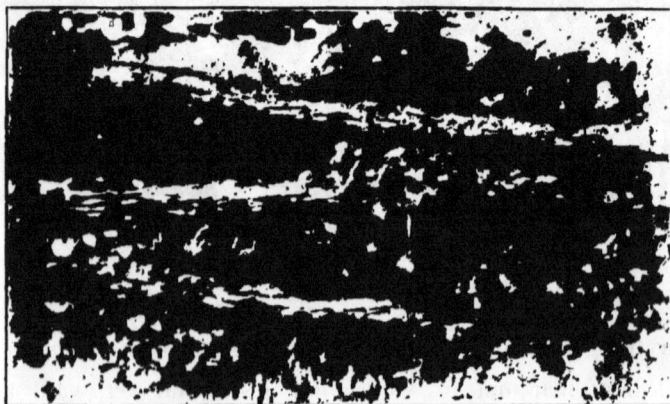

THE UNDER CAT.

The poets have sung in lofty strains,
  Likewise all the sages doth write.
In high-toned verses, with tears bedewed,
  'Bout the under dog in the fight.
They'll tell you, in deep concern, the wrong
  Of strong over weak, and that,
But never a whimper you'll get from them,
  When you talk of the uppermost cat.

To those who watch these felines " scrap,"
  In their noisy, boisterous ways,
Observe that victory's not to the strong,
  But to wise old Tom who lays
Upon his back, with claws unsheathed,
  His eyes with green fire alight —
Shed tears for the uppermost cat, but bet
  On the under cat in the fight.

The air will be full of long drawn sighs,
  With vision of claws and fur,
With spittings and cussings, world 'thout end,
  But with them nary a purr.
You may talk of your " knock-out " slugging bees,
  Your bicycle races and walks,
The rowing of boats, or shooting of guns,
  For the under cat, " my money talks."

There's joy in the battle's roar, they say,
  But I'd rather take their word,
For I 'spose it makes some difference
  Where you stand, when it is heard ;
But just for pure enjoyment, like,
  'Thout risk of life or limb,
Is to watch two felines wage a war,
  And the under cat — bet on him !

It's lots of fun, they tell me, too,
  When track and weather's fine,
To watch the face of the knowing man,
  Who has bet on the wrong equine,
How he does cuss his own bad luck,
  While the winner throws his hat
High in the air, with lusty shout –
  You see, he's the under cat.

This life is mainly a battle for bread,
  For raiment, shelter and rest ;
And happy is he who can laugh at fate,
  When he comes out second best,
The earth he knows turns o'er and o'er,
  In its never-wearying flight,
And he smiles to think that half the time
  He's the under cat in the fight.

PLAIN JANE AND ME.

I allus keered fer fancy names, er sech as sounded well,
A slippin' smoothly from the tongue Cath'rine er Isabel,
Isadora, Wilhelmine, Hellena, Josephine,
Er Hanner, er Susanner, 'Lizabeth, er Imogene,
Till I saw an awe-inspirin' girl, with her head well up in air,
An' a kinder look which seemed to say: " Jest tech me, if you
        dare ! "
My theories all took to flight my heart thumped lustily,
An' acknowledged that plain Jane was good enough fer me !

Of course she was superior anybody could see that,
By the upward tipping of her nose to match her jaunty hat;
An' the way she put her foot down, as she walked along the
        way,
Servin' notice on the men folks that 'twas goin' down to stay,
How I trimbled when I took her hand, an' with lover's down
        cast eyes,
Asked the question she expected with a look of feigned surprise
Chewed her handkercher a minit an' what she said, you see,
Will never be reported by either Jane or me !

Apple blossoms are as pretty as the orange fer a bride,
An' everybody thought so, as she towered by my side,
So self possessed an' conscious, so smilin' an' so sweet
An' I all of a trimble, an' could scarcely keep my feet;

An' the crowd there all a gigglin' within the festive hall —
But I saw 'em kinder misty-like, if any way at all :
" Will you have this 'ere woman ? " the preacher sez, sez he ;
An' I murmured that " plain Jane was good enough fer me ! "

Life's jest a streak of sunshine, bordered all along the way ;
While flowers nod approval, where'er my feet may stray,
A lightin' up the narrow path with colors warm an' bright —
But I know now how the moon feels, shinin' with reflected light !
I haint a braggin' of it, though I'm glad to make a note
Of the fact that I am privileged to go an' cast a vote :
But the honor seems an empty one, for I reckon that to be
The husband of plain Jane is good enough fer me !

She belongs to all the Wimmen's Clubs, an' my ! she knows
        a heap !
She can't tell all she knows by day, so talks it in her sleep ;
In her hungerin's fer knowledge an' improvin' of herself,
She spends hours readin' papers she lays on the pantry shelf.
Proudest moments in my life, sence the hour I first knew her,
Is when she sets an' talks to me 'sif I was ekal to her !
Sech picters in home life these days are beautiful to see —
So I reckon that plain Jane is good enough fer me !

She can make a mustard plaster, bringin' water to the eye ;
Sendin' a feller's memory to the middle of July —
Er make a flax seed poultice as soft as summer's rain,
An' as soothin' as the echo of music's sweetest strain.
I haint no cause to grumble, even if she did diskiver
That stiddy work is jest the thing fer a feller's lazy liver ;
An' ef she does the docterin', that's the way its got to be,
Fer I reckon that plain Jane knows what is best fer me !

OCTOBER.

She is coming ! She is coming !
  Crowned with leaves of crimson dye,
With grape stains on her beauteous lips,
  And laughter in her eye ;
Dodging the fast falling nuts,
  Jack Frost is scattering free,
While fire, unconsuming, rests
  On every bush and tree ;
With smoke-veiled face now smiling o'er us,
  Our dear October stands before us !

THE WORLD'S FAIR POEM.

I'm very much obleeged to you for your flatterin' invite,
To write a poem for the Fair and be there to recite ;
I'm purty bizzy these ere days, me and my hired man,
But I'll think it over keerful like, and do the best I can.

It's quite unlucky that I sent Pegassus out to graze :
For portry in the " wild and woolly " hardly ever pays ;
I 'spose that I can coax him back if he haint gone too far —
Ef not, I reckon I can hitch my wagon to a star !

When inspiration's skeery like, the writin' of a piece,
Is not, as ginerally supposed, to be " as slick as grease ; "
It's purty nigh as tough a job, as it would seem to me,
As twistin' a shriekin' rabbit outen a holler tree !

I've had that World's Fair on my mind purty nigh day and night,
A fearin', that, like Moses, I might die without the sight ;
But now I read my title clear — am one of the elect,
Jest so to speak and I'll be there, at least I so expect.

Mirandy says I'll hev to git a new outfit of clothes ;
Trousers, vest, Prince Albert coat — and what else, goodness knows ;

And she's also of the 'pinion that I will look the best,
Wearin' a sash to hide the gap 'twixt onfriendly pants and vest !

I've been a worryin', in my mind, 'bout sellin' off some stock ;
I 'spose I must, at some price, or else I'll hev to walk
And countin' ties in these 'ere days is everlastin' slow,
So I 'spose the tailless Jersey cow and calf will hev to go !

If the People's Party was in power, 'twould be an easy trick
To turn our projuce into cash most everlastin' quick ;
Fer the gov'ment would be ready, jest as soon as we could
    thrash,
To git out papers on our grain so's we could git the cash.

Er, if we had a lot of cows, or a onruly bull,
Er some scabby sheep, er goats, er a hoss that wouldn't pull,
We could send 'em to the gov'ment, by one of our smart lads,
Who'd tie 'em to the treas'ry fence and go in fer the scads !

Jest what they'd want of onery bulls is more'n I can tell ;
But they hev 'em down on Wall Street, why not Washington
    as well ?
Mebbe next Congress may be slow, as last one was, I learn,
They'll turn 'em in there   jest as an inducement to adjourn.

I'm glad you're goin' to hev some things that can't be found at
    home :
Some " Sacred Cats " from Egypt, and some " Catacombs " from
    Rome,
And ef the show is carried out accordin' to programs,
You'll hev there Ancient Rameses   and other Batterin' Rams !

Rameses was a 'Gyptian King and one of his smart tricks
Was to slip down to the brickyards and count the Hebrews'
        bricks ;
He stepped on 'em with both his feet — but Powderly was there,
And as he wouldn't arbitrate, he'll bring him to the Fair !

I'll try and git there in good time. to take in all the show,
I've kinder mapped out in my mind jest where I wanter go —
I don't know which will be most fun — a minglin' with the races
Er a watchin' them New Yorkers comin' in a makin' faces !

THE RELUCTANT IDEA.

Her head was resting on one hand,
    The other held a pen ;
She dipped it deep, in violet ink,
    Glanced at the ceiling then ;
And sighing, cried aloud to space :
" Not since the days of Cicero,
    Nor since the world was framed, I know,
Have new ideas come so slow ! "
    Forgetting, in her deep distress,
    Her new style " graduating dress ! "

THE RACE AT CHEROKEE.

Say, what you fellers laughin' at ? I reckon you have guessed
I'm a silver miner from the State way out in the West,
Where the Governor wished to wade in gore up to his bridle
    reins,
An' to fight ter silver jest as long as the blood stayed in his
    veins.
Mebbe et you'd been where I hev, an' knowed what I've been
    through,
A sleepin' out of nights, an' a feelin' kinder blue
At the slim chances to git a homestead, don't you see
I'm jest back from the races down thar in Cherokee !

It beat a hen a peckin', to see the people, when
They gathered in from every place, from every nook an' glen,
An' girded tightly up their loins to run a race fer land.
Fer which, up here in Iowa, you wouldn't turn your hand.
There was women, men an' Injuns, a waitin' ter the day,
Fer the signal to be given, fer all to rush away
Across the line to mingle in a strugglin' human sea,
In the wild race fer a homestead, down thar in Cherokee !

There was Missourians an' Texans, Kansas men in large amount —
I represented Iowa, as near as I kin count —
All mounted upon wagons, horses, mustangs, or on mules,
Loaded down with cookin' implements and lots of shootin' tools,
All a swearin' an' a growlin' an' a scrougin' all about,
A waitin' for the pistol shots — the signal to rush out.
Not long ago I read how Sherman marched down to the sea
That was a picnic, though, compared to the race at Cherokee.

When the signal gun was fired, you'd orter see the sight,
As us hundred thousand boomers betook ourselves to flight;
How we tumbled o'er each other, in our wild and mad career,
As we lashed our horses till they ran with speed of frightened
        deer;
One woman, who, upon her back, had strapped her little tot,
Made a gallant race, and fairly won a valuable lot;
She sat there with baby as happy as could be - -
She'd got jest what she'd come for, in the race at Cherokee.

'Leven bicycle fellers took the road agin' the field, an' won it;
They rode " Des Moines Pacemakers," or they never could a
        done it.
Them chaps could beat the fastest train, I spose, as well as not;
They humped themselves that time, for sure, an' each one got a
        lot.
The " sooners," the sworn deputies, an' the gov'ment's favored
        horde
Got in a few hours previous an' nearly swept the board,
By goblin' up the choicest lots an' landed property,
So the stiddy goers all got left in the race at Cherokee.

Me? Git anything? I guess not; I rode a kickin' mule.
An' he stopped to kick at everything, the ornery old fool !
Didn't git thar till noon next day   at every wayside station
I met some people comin' back a cussin' the administration
For carryin' the cruel joke much furder than it orter,
An' washin' disappointments down with government salt worter;
Don't know how it struck other folks   that's the way it 'peared
        to me.
As I look back on the races down thar in Cherokee.

Well, yes, that's so, jest as you say, Of course it mought have
        been.
But 'fore I got thar all the mayors was 'lected an' sworn in,
An' houses built in all the towns. They do things thar much
        quicker
'Taint the fust time a candidate's been knocked out by a kicker !
Iowa's good enough for me. I'll camp here, sure's yer born
Say, know where I could strike a stiddy job of shuckin' corn ?
An', would you mind a puttin' up a plain, square meal for me ?
Haint had one sence I lost the race down thar in Cherokee.

"Edge Water," overlooking Highland Park, a favorite spot of the Author, and where many of these poems were written.

FORTY YEARS IN IOWA.

1855 - 1895.

Forty years in Iowa ! How curious it seems ;
Like the passing years of fancy, or the mistiest of dreams !
To look back from this Mizpah, at the swiftly flying years,
Marked with more of joy than sorrow, with more of smiles than
    tears !
To look back on the changes, for the better, it may be,
To the straggling, dirty village, to the city which we see.
Friends tell us that she's smokier than ever ! Fie, for shame !
Clean or dirty, she will ever be my sweetheart, just the same.

Suppose the smoke-clouds stand above, as in the days of old,
To mark the tabernacle, and the sacred tent enfold ;
It means Prosperity some day, will settle down to stay,
And fill the place with factories which will not run away !
Would that it were thicker : and a thousand factory throats
Were belching it from lofty stacks, to their whistles' noisy notes ;
We know the soot and grime 'twould bring but with it comes
        the hope
Of swelling purses, making it the easier to buy soap !

Forty years in Iowa ! And the changes they have wrought,
To swell her growing triumph ! Ah, who ever thought
As he plodded through the mire, in a desultory way,
He would travel dry shod over bricks made from this very clay !
Who could have faintly pictured then, the glory of a home
'Neath the shadow and the glitter of the Capitol's bright dome ;
Or swap slow stage for railroad, bringing commerce from afar ;
Or harness up chained lightning to the swiftly moving car !

Forty years in Iowa ! And the friends we've gathered here !
How these golden links are strengthened, with every rolling year !
Tilts and quarrels may have sometimes embittered every cup
But the " Spirit of Des Moines " says ; " Kiss and make it up."
Cheer up and sing your peans to the State we hold most dear,
Which celebrates her fiftieth anniversary next year.
Get on your knees and ask the Lord to let you see that day
And don't forget to thank Him for a home in Iowa !

Forty years in Iowa ! This maid when " sweet sixteen,"
Sent out one hundred thousand sons the bravest ever seen
To save a Nation and a Flag vile hands had fastened on,
And wrote their characters in blood at Shiloh, Donelson,
At Wilson's Creek, at Corinth, from " Atlanta to the Sea,"

And home by way of Richmond — as proud as proud could be !
They brought " Old Glory " with them which not a son dis-
    graced - -
Faded, and torn, and tattered but not a star displaced !

Forty years in Iowa ! Where Peace and Plenty walk ;
While Famine, sore, and Hunger, outside her borders stalk.
Ah, who can speak the glories of this Queen, with Plenty's horn,
As she sits to bless the nations, from her throne of golden corn !
And who may tell the future of the many years in store,
When her name, her fame, her goodness, are sung from shore to
    shore.
As a land of sun-kissed prairies, where Plenty ever reigns -
There's no hurry about Heaven, while Iowa remains !

SHE HAD.

" Didst e'er contribute for the press ? "
    Asked the editor with smile,
  Looking in her bright blue eyes,
    Her hand in his, the while.
" Oh, yes," she said, with interest deep,
    And face with blushes bright ;
" I often do — that is to say,
    By turning down the light ! "

HOOSIER RECOLLECTIONS.

I reckon I am jest about as old-fashioned as can be,
  An' kinder hanker after good, old-fashioned things :
Old-fashioned songs and stories   an', so far as I can see,
  The good old way of courtin', an' the style of weddin' rings.
I've allus had an idee, that, in the good old way
  Of puttin' on a weddin' ring in such a solemn style,
Twould last longer an' cling closter, than the style in vogue to-
    day,
  When promises are lightly made for such a little while.

I git to thinkin', sometimes, an' questionin' myself,
  An' askin': " Are we happy as in days gone by,
When livin' was more simple, an' the mad pursuit of pelf
  Did not absorb our bein's ? " An' my answer is a sigh.
Is there a Hoosier living, who would willin'ly exchange
  The ager for the microbes, the bacteria or gout,
That you swaller with your vittles, or take in at short range,
  Through your breathin' apparatus, to eat your vitals out ?

Jest think of it a minute ! In the good, old-fashioned days,
  The doctors had plain names for diseases of all sorts :
They mixed calomel an' jalap in the most enticin' ways,
  An' tackled ailments boldly, from pneumonia to warts.

In these days of swift progression, our physicians do not grope
  In the dark as did our doctors ; for if they have a doubt.
They light up our interiors, as long as there is hope,
  To see jest what is in us — an' try to knock it out !

I 'spose I've laughed a thousand times 'bout the old style of
    courtin'
  The boys an' girls accomplished by the fireplace, long an' wide,
While the unsnuffed taller candle. its sputterin' wick disportin',
  Threw shadders dim, upon the wall. of the couple side by side.
With taller dips fer sparkin', 'lectricity isn't in it.
  When safety and convenience are the things you talk about ;
If they ever got too brilliant, it only took a minnit
  To rise to the occasion an' gently snuff 'em out !

I think the style of kissin' in a small room is the worst,
  Which sounds like the quick drawin' of a colt's foot from the
    mud :
Givin' parents the impression that the yeast bottle has burst,
  As it breaks upon the stillness with a loud resoundin' thud.
I miss the old well sweep. with its salutations bowin',
  As it brought the drippin' bucket from the waters cool below,
With the hollyhocks, the poppies, an' the tall sunflowers growin'
  By the well side where I've slaked my thirst so many years
    ago.

My heart goes out in hunger for the great. wide spreading beech
    wood.
  An' poplars. with their winged seeds. around my cabin door ;
An' troopin' back to mem'ry comes the dear old spot where each
    stood.
  To wave its giant arms above my happy home of yore.

Then there was " apple cuttin's," an' the sports which came
    soon after,
  An' playin' " Sister Phoebe," in the mellow candle light ;
Er " Marchin' down to Quebec," with a mouth chock full of
    lafter ;
  As it comes back to me to-day 'twas simply " out of sight ! "

Mebbe to the fiddle's sound, the boys an' girls would mingle,
  In the chaste and merry dances so well known in days of yore,
With ruddy cheeks aglow, while their very feet would tingle
  As they spoke their rythmic pleasure upon the puncheon floor.
As life's shadders fade away on the paths pressed by our feet,
  Dear Friends, may it be your great happiness an' mine,
To sound our golden harps with a joyousness complete,
  As the notes we blew on trumpet made of punkin vine !

SEPTEMBER.

Now blooms the feath'ry goldenrod,
    The flower of Iowa's choice ;
The katydid and cricket, too,
    Have lifted up their voice.
The works of Nature, careless-like,
    Are strewn in woods and field,
Spread out in a September sun,
    With every book unsealed.

CHRISTMAS DOINGS.

Old Christmas is a comin' ! You kin feel it in the air,
Fer our wimin folks are a workin' on the sly an' wond'rin' where
They can hide their precious secrets, where no pryin' eye can see--
An' there's not a man on top of ground that's tickelder than me !
It's jest a little techin', though --an' not a little fun
To hev a pair of slippers, er ear kivers, when they're done.
As to be so very liberal regardin' length and size,
As to cause the veriest donkey a sweet an' glad surprise.

An' the children ! Bless the children, with their brains all in a
   whirl
Don't forget 'em. There is love enough for every boy an' girl
If sorted out by lovin' hearts an' willin' hands, to bless
All the world, on this glad day of self-forgetfulness.
Let yer mem'ry take a short cut : my ! how quickly old Time
   slips ;
Only yest'day you kissed yer mother with yer taffy-covered lips,
A wond'rin' who Old Santa was, who knew yer wants so well,
Feelin' sure that papa knew him — if he would only tell.

An' I used to wonder how it was, when chimbleys were so small,
How Santa Claus could find the place an' leave presents fer us
   all
An' jest the things we prayed fer, too when childish hearts
   were stirred.

In tones so loud an' earnest, parents must have overheard.
I hope that all the boys an' girls will be found by good Old
    Santa,
Whether they dwell in mansions large, or live in a small shanty ;
An' may I express a hope of him   I'm sure he will not mind it,
That there'll be no chimbly in this land so small but he will
    find it !

A memory rises here, an' in happy, boyish mood,
I sit at grandpa's table in an Indianny wood,
In a double hewed log cabin in the middle of a clearin'
Which grandma allus spoke of as bein' " out of sight an' hearin',"
A Christmas feast ! A pig well browned, with an apple in his
    jaws,
Which he didn't seem to care for, or take interest in, because
If grandpa did the carvin', he would slice him in a minit
An' I allus got the piece that had the kidneys in it.

Then there was a big fat gobbler, roasted before the fire,
Hitched to a cabin cross beam with a strong cord spliced with
    wire,
An' it hung there jest a whirlin', as if 'twould never stop
An' the iron pan beneath it, caught the gravy, drop by drop.
The table was jest loaded   an' there was no bill of fare
That you had to read all over 'fore you knowed jest what was
    there :
Grandpa allus ast a blessin'   he generally said :
" Oh, Lord, we thank Thee, (mumble, mumble,) Sally, pass the
    bread ! "

An' grandma'd say : " Jest reach in an' take out, fer pap an' me
Aint either of us any hands to wait on company,"
She allus was pretendin' like her cookin' was so pore !
An' yet she'd keep a urgin' us to take a little more

Said the turkey, it was underdone, an' the biscuits was burnt
   black,
An' all the hull endurin' day there was something out of whack ;
An' she hoped that we could somehow make a dinner of sech
   stuff · -
Grandpa allus raised both eyebrows when we said we'd et enuff !

An' there we'd sit an' laugh an' joke all Christmas afternoon,
Er grandpa'd git his fiddle out an' play a lively tune,
So full of joy an' sweetness as would dispel all earthly woes,
An' make a feller wonder what had got into his toes !
In fiddlin'. grandpa allus took the middle of the road ;
When he began to play a tune then everybody knowed
It was a fight clean to the finish, fer he sawed it through an'
   through,
Nor skirmished round the aiges like our modern fiddlers do !

Christmas may come an' Christmas go, but love is jest the same,
An' will outlive all things on earth, from riches up to fame ;
But memory, sweet, will linger on the good old Christmas times
An' contrast them - not unkindly — with our faster ringin' chimes,
An' drop a kindly tear for those whose love will ne'er decay,
Who are with us in the spirit on this merry Christmas day ;
Whose hearts have throbbed with love for all without a restin'
   spell
For eighty-five or ninety years hope ours will do as well !

RECONSIDERATION.

I wooed the Muse with sweetest dalliance,
  And asked it she would strike the tuneful lyre,
Which, in my breast, lay voiceless or, perchance,
  Waiting her finger's touch of poetic fire ;
But she, in scorn refused, with haughty brow,
  And gave me no encouragement at all,
But said : " Why should I walk with such as thou,
  Whose sleeve ne'er rubbed inside a college wall ? "

In silent grief, I turned to homely Prose,
  Who sat apart with modest, downcast eyes ;
" Wilt walk with me ? " I faltered. For reply she rose,
  And hand in hand, we wandered 'neath the skies,
Where rivulets sang of Love ; and where
  Willows laved their thirsty boughs ; where bees
With drowsy hum, and song birds charmed the air
  With sweetest music, 'mid the Linden trees.

We stood where mountain torrents roared and rushed,
  Foaming and impatient, as they sped away ;
Or watched the eastern glow, where morn first blushed,
  Or saw the angels put up the bars of day.
We walked where fancy or inclination pressed,
  In sweet communion, as spake mind to mind ;
But not alone, for you may well have guessed
  The jealous Muse came tagging on behind !

THE POET OF THE FUTURE.

" Oh, the poet of the future ! Will he come to us as comes
The beauty of the bugle's voice above the roar of drums
The beauty of the bugle's voice above the roar and din
Of battle drums that pulse the time the victor marches in ? "
                                            --JAMES WHITCOMB RILEY.

" Oh, the poet of the future ! " Can anybody guess
Whether he'll sound his bugle, or she'll wear them on her dress ;
An' will thev kinder get their themes from natur', second hand.
An' dish 'em up in language plain folks can't understand ?

There's a sight of this 'ere portry stuff. every year. that goes to
        waste,
Jest a waitin' fer a poet. who has the time an' taste.
To tackle it jest as it is. an' weave it into rhyme,
With warp an' woof of Hope an' Love. in Life's swift loom of
        time.

An'. mebbe the futur' poet. ef he knows everything,
Will not start the summer katydids to singin' in the spring.
Jest like the croakin frog ; but let the critter wait at most,
To announce to timid farmer. that " It's jest six weeks to frost."

The katydid an' goldenrod are pardners in this way,
They sing an' bloom where'er there's room, along Life's sunny
        way ;

So I warn you, futur' poet, jest let 'em bloom an' lilt
Together. Don't divorce 'em. That's jest the way they're built.

In order to be perfect, the futur' poet should
Know every sound of natur', of river, lake an' wood ;
Should know each whispered note an' every answerin' call
He should never set cock pheasants to drummin' in the fall

" Under the golden maples ! " Not havin' voice to sing,
They flap their love out on a log quite early in the spring ;
For burnin' love will allus find expression in some way
That's the style they have adopted   don't change their natur's,
          pray !

I cannot guess jest what the futur' poet's themes may be ;
Reckon they'll be pretty lofty, fer any one can see
That the world of portry's lookin' up an' poets climbin' higher ;
With divine afflatus boostin' 'em, of course, they must aspire.

The poets of the good old times were cruder with the pen ;
Their idees wern't the same as ours   those good old-fashioned
          men
Bet old Homer never writ, even in his palmiest day,
Such a soul-upliftin' poem as " Hosses Chawin' Hay ! "

" Hosses " don't know no better, out in the Hawkeye State
Down to Bosting, now, I reckon, they jest simply masticate.
The poet of the futur'll blow a bugle, like as not
Most all us modern poets had to blow fer all we've got ;

To keep the pot a bilin', we all hev to raise a din,
To make the public look our way   an' pass the shekels in.
The scarcity of bugles seem now the greatest lack
Though some of us keep blowin' 'thout a bugle to our back !

The poet of the futur' ! When once he takes his theme,
His pen will slip as smoothly as a canoe glides down a stream
He'll sing from overflowin' heart - his music will be free —
Would you take up a subscription for a robin in a tree ?

He'll never try to drive the Muse, if she doesn't want to go :
But will promptly take her harness off   er drive keerfully an'
      slow - -
When portry's forced, like winter pinks, the people's apt to know
      it
An' labor with it jest about as hard as did the poet !

CAUSE AND EFFECT.

Cause and Effect went out for a walk,
   On a tour of observation,
And filled up the time with sociable talk.
   Regarding their close relation.
A buzz saw was speeding in silence around.
   Looking harmless as harmless could be
" It's buzzing ! " said Cause. " It is not ! " said Effect,
" At least, I am going to see ! "
When whish ! There's no man who ever yet knew
What buzz saws or the New Woman will do !

A RIVER IDYL

A RIVER IDYL.

How sweet it is, to idly float,
  On waters strange, in sun and dew;
To hear the wild bird's joyous note,
  While cruising, in a staunch canoe.
What joy to follow Nature's bent,
  Where roses wild, perfume the air;
To mingle with grape blossoms scent,
  And breathe in Nature everywhere!

A cruise down an unknown river is one of the delights of life to one who is in love with Nature and wishes to court her in her various moods, for it gives one an opportunity to get away from the busy haunts of men and have a chance in the quiet of the woods, by great shadows of overhanging cliffs, or on the sweet-voiced river, to think. How pleasant it is in this busy world to have a week in which to do up your thinking for a year.

In a canoe, you sit facing the situation, on an air cushion, if you like, while at your back is another cushion, harder or softer as desired, while your feet are braced against a foot rest at a proper distance to give you a position of solidity. With a double bladed paddle, you can send your light, dainty little craft in any direction you please, or you can lay your paddle across the coam-

ing in front of you and let her find her own way down the
current, while you read or sketch.

In answer to the universal question asked by those unfamiliar
with cruising canoes : " Do they upset easily ? " I will say they
do not. A skillful canoeist is seldom, if ever, capsized while
paddling. He sits low in the canoe and balances himself, as it
were, by intuition. The paddle, also, assists in steadying the
canoe in running rapids, or in rough water. A canoe will live
in any water which is safe for a row boat if the canoeist has
nerve and a fair amount of muscle. Accidents will sometimes
happen : in which case do not desert your craft. All cruising
canoes have air-tight compartments which will float you and your
cargo until you can get safely to shore.

On June 15, 1892, by the kindness of W. H. Quick, of the
United States Express, a gentleman who was never known to
forget a friend, and the courtesy of the manager and officers of
the Minneapolis & St. Louis Railroad, Mr. Walter Weatherley, of
the canoe, " Tumsie," and Tac Hussey, of the canoe, " Dab-
chick," were kindly allowed to place their canoes in the baggage
car for a run to Humboldt, Iowa, from which point a cruise was
to be made of about two hundred miles down the Des Moines
River.

The country over which this road passes is very beautiful and
what with the prairies, with their verdure and variegated flowers,
the tintings of earth and sky, the promise of bountiful crops, it
was a panorama which could only bring peace and contentment
to every heart. The road runs for some distance along the upper
Des Moines and the two canoeists saw, with much gratification the
silver track, rippling and dancing in the June sun, upon which
they would soon be taking their downward course home. The
destination reached, the canoes, by the kindness of the Russell
House proprietors, were placed in the sample room, which is on
the ground floor. The canoe tents were put in place, the cushions and air pillows blown up and left to the inspection of the

public, and of which privilege many ladies and gentlemen promptly availed themselves. I wish to say a good word here for the boys of Humboldt. The rooms were left open all the afternoon, and there were a great many boy visitors, who asked many questions, which were courteously answered. They handled nothing, and not so much as a piece of cord was missing. On coming back to see if all was right after a short walk about town, I found a little four or five-year-old girl snugly ensconced in my canoe, sitting in state on the cushions, her little head against the cushioned back-board. She explained, on being discovered, as she looked up trustingly, that she was " taking a little boat vide," and she was left in full command. How far she sailed, or how long she continued her imaginary cruise, I know not.

The citizens of Humboldt are a very genial, social people, and we got all the necessary information in regard to river and dams. Mr. Joseph McCauley, especially, gave some good pointers on fishing, as he is the champion fisherman of that section.

On Thursday morning, after all needed supplies were purchased, the canoes were sent to the west branch of the river, near the creamery. Quite an interest was excited in seeing the dainty little crafts loaded. Each one had a cargo of at least seventy-five pounds, and it seemed to puzzle the onlookers to know where it was all to be stowed and yet leave room for the crews. One gentleman begged that we would not start until he had assembled his family on the bridge to see the departure. All the " duffle," as canoeists term it, was safely stowed so as to trim, the painters were loosed, and, with the crews aboard, the canoes shot down the swift current with only an occasional stroke of the paddle to guide. Good-byes were said, hands and handkerchiefs were waived, as the bridge was passed and the rapid current soon bore us out on the two hundred mile cruise homeward.

How beautiful is this west branch of the Des Moines ! Narrow, swift, bounded by high, rocky shores, and running over a

rough, rocky bed, full of rapids, the roar of which could be
heard for a mile. The scenery is wild and picturesque, sometimes
a rocky cliff, sometimes a spreading, rocky beach, covered with
trees, vine clad, and wild roses everywhere. Some of the rapids
were a fourth of a mile long, and the turbulent waters tossed
the plunging canoes like corks, now dipping their noses under
water and throwing the spray high in the air as they rose from
the plunge. It is estimated that these rapids run at the rate of
eight miles an hour, and the shooting of them would be a dangerous experiment in a time of low water.

There is nothing in canoeing so exhiliarating as shooting a
rapid. The nerves must be steady, the eye quick and the hand
ready. As a general thing, a canoe will find her way, but she
must be kept " head on," for in striking a rock sidewise, the
force of the current would capsize you in much less time than it
takes to tell it. There are probably twenty-five of these rapids,
large and small, including broken dams, between Humboldt and
Fort Dodge, none of which are dangerous except in a low stage
of water.

The west and east branches of the river form a junction about
nine miles below Humboldt and it becomes wider, yet by no
means less wild. The forests become more dense, the rocky
cliffs higher, and the river, in some places, looks as if it had
cut its channel through solid rock. Nature is a tireless worker
and a few thousand years makes no especial difference to her in
the completion of a piece of handiwork. Boulders, weighing many
tons, are to be found in the channel, around and over which the
waters rush and roar. Occasionally a large piece of the cliff has
become detached and falling into the channel would form an
obstruction over which the angry water would surge and hiss,
forming miniature whirpools, beating the water into a white foam.

When the water becomes clear the upper part of this river
will be a paradise to fishermen. A few casts of an artificial fly
were rewarded by a fine, three-pound, wall-eyed pike, which

made an excellent dinner for two, with something to spare. Later in the day, some bass were taken, and in the evening, a three and a half pound pickerel was caught on a Buel spinning bait. As the cast was made from a high rock, he had to be tired out before he could be landed at a point considerably above, where a shelving rock reached down to the water's edge. He made several high leaps in his fight for liberty, but as he was firmly hooked, a springy rod did the rest.

The encampment was made that night in a very pretty spot, opposite a high bluff. A cold stream ran out of the hill into the river and made a handy place to stow our milk and butter after the evening meal had been cooked and eaten. A farm house near at hand supplied the milk for a small consideration and the two voyagers were happy. The canoes were " shored up," that is, they were placed on an even keel in a level spot on the bank and sticks of right length were placed under the beading to hold them in that position, a quantity of feathery willow leaves and twigs were strewn in the bottom, over which rubber blankets were spread, then the cushions were placed thereon, the air pillows blown up, the under and upper woolen blankets were put in position, the canoe tents hung on the two masts and buttoned down on the sides of the canoes, a mosquito bar thrown over each door to guard against unwelcome visitors and climbing in they went to sleep amid the perfume of wild grape blossoms, wild roses, and the music of the whip-poor-wills.

Did you ever hear one of these birds sing within a few yards of you ? They make a peculiar little noise before beginning their song which I can only liken to the whirring of a clock before it strikes, after which they repeat their song from ten to eighty-five times, by actual count. Then, after a few seconds' rest, the whirring sound is again made and the song proceeds. Many people regard the song as a mournful or sorrowful one. To me, it is one of the pleasantest, on account of its plaintive earnestness and general desire to be social.

Next morning we were awakened at day light by the snort-
ings of a frightened horse. He had evidently come down to the
river's bank to drink, and seeing the canoe tents in the uncertain
light of early morning became so affrighted that he plunged into
the river and swam for dear life to the other side, giving a farewell snort as he clambered up the rocky bank and disappeared
in the woods. An hour after, the coffee was boiling, the bacon
was frying and a hearty breakfast was made, preparatory to a
start on the downward course. A fog veiled the river until nine
o'clock, while the high bluffs and forest trees were lightly kissed
by the sun, turning them to burnished silver.

The river, as Fort Dodge is approached, is very wild ; rocky,
with high cliffs, from which the wild grape vine clings and the
wild rose blooms in every available place. Large bouquets were
gathered and placed in the forward mast tubes where they shed
a grateful fragrance and delighted the eye at short range. The
wild rose is one of the wild-wood beauties which appeal to the
human heart. They seem to take delight in making glad the
desert and waste places. Sometimes they were found growing from
between clefts of rock where there seemed to be no soil or support, and yet they clung and bloomed sweetly in the face of all
difficulties, whether the eye of man ever enjoyed their beauty and
fragrance or not. In the morning, they are a beautiful, bright
pink ; at noon, a lighter pink, and at evening, the leaves are
blanched and ready to fall a life of beauty and fragrance for
only one day. No one will deny that they perform God's mission well, in seen and unseen spots. Is not this a lesson to
mortals, that wherever their lots are cast, the perfume of their
lives in good words and works may ever be ready to cheer the
passer-by on the journey of life ?

A steady roar far down the stream told us that we were
approaching a dam or rapids. It proved to be the ruins of a dam
a few miles above Fort Dodge. Some workmen who were quar-
rying rock shouted to us to go to the other side, where there

was less fall, but we did not think it prudent to change our course, so our staunch little crafts plunged over the three feet fall, burying their noses in the foam, but shipping not a drop of water as they dashed down the cataract like mad, to the amazement of the onlookers, who, no doubt, supposed the little crafts would be swamped.

Sometimes there would be quite a long stretch of river with a sharp turn to right or left, and from a distance it would look as if the stream terminated then and there, but on approaching the bend, the way would be unfolded as if by magic and the course made plain. I could not help thinking how much it resembled, in this respect, the stream of life, down which all are cruising, some listlessly, some thoughtfully, and some beset with fears within and without. There come times in many lives when the way seems shut up, when the sky overhead is as brass and the dew of heaven falls not. Yet they who go forward hopefully, cheerfully and trustfully will ever find a way for their goings.

Fort Dodge was reached about nine o'clock. A rumor had been started in some way that two Indians were coming down the river in canoes, and quite a company had assembled near Heath's oat meal mill to see the sight. By some miscalculation or inattention to business, I allowed my canoe to drift on a sand bar and had the humiliating privilege of taking off my shoes and stockings and towing her to deeper water. A landing was made at the wagon bridge, and the first man to greet us was our old townsman, H. R. Heath. Two hours were spent in getting some supplies and looking over Heath's magnificent oat meal mill, which is the pride of Fort Dodge, and calling on a few acquaintances.

Fort Dodge is a pretty, thriving little town, with abundant material for every kind of a factory. You can find anything here, from limestone rock to material from which to make a " Cardiff Giant." Adjutant General Baker once explained the formation of this wonderfully diversified region by saying that " when the

Lord finished making the earth. He had a few odds and ends of all kinds left over, so they were dumped out at Fort Dodge."

Again on board, the canoes were allowed to drift down the swift current, while the canoeists lay back on the cushions with sighs of calm enjoyment. For miles the river has sloping, grassy banks, strewn, here and there, with boulders. Amid stream, great rocks lay, partially submerged, around which the current rushed in many circling eddies. Some of them were eight or ten feet in diameter, the relics of the glacier period, when mountains of ice, thousands of feet thick, ground mountains of rock into boulders as they moved on their way south at the rate of four or five inches a day during the millions of years the earth was being prepared as a battle ground for wealth and preferment for ever greedy man.

Everywhere, from the beginning to the end of the journey, was displayed the wonderful power of water. Thousands of forest trees were uprooted and seemed as straws when the flood was at its height, as they were undermined and laid in rows where the river made a sharp turn and rushed across to the next bend. Sometimes the flood became humorous and played fanciful tricks with drift wood and debris. At the top of an immense drift, at one of the bends, a small tree was lodged which drooped gracefully twenty feet above the water. Upon this tree was a kitchen chair, in its natural position, swaying to and fro in the breeze. It is estimated that to have placed that pile of drift wood in position and crowned its summit with a chair, so airily poised, would have cost a gang of men a week's work and more profanity than to have put up a twelve-jointed stove pipe in the presence of a suggestive wife !

A camp that night was made on an island. It was also strewn with debris. The nail kegs found there made a beautiful camp fire, but the cart wheel, horse collar and boy's wool hat could not be utilized. We slept the sleep of the tired that night, to the music of the water on all sides and the never failing whip-poor-will on either shore, enhanced, no doubt, by a thorough bath from one of the pebbly shores. Mosquitos were very numerous in the woods and on the river, but when the canoe tents were in position, closely buttoned down to the sides of the canoes and the netting hung across the doors, the mosquitos were not in it with us.

There is not, to a hungry man, a more appetizing smell than that which comes from boiling coffee and frying bacon. When it is done crisp and brown, break your eggs and cook them slowly, turn them, if you like them that way, and with brown bread and butter, you have a breakfast fit for a king. I am sure you are anxious to know how the coffee was settled. There was no settling to do. Small bags of cheese cloth were provided by a thoughtful wife, and the water was put on cold, with the proper amount of coffee in the little sack, and that was all there was to it. When it came to a boil, it was set on another part of the fire to simmer gently until everything else was ready to serve up. The washing of the frying pan has always been looked upon as an irksome task. In camp, it was a pleasure. So soon as the frying is done, fill the frying pan with clean, dry sand and let it stand until the meal is finished. The sand has, by that time, absorbed all the grease and a vigorous rubbing with a dry rag and fine sand will make it shine like a mirror and remove every particle of unpleasant odor. Tin plates, knives, forks and spoons will yield to the same kind of treatment, except that the application need not be so vigorously applied.

Canoes launched, loaded and we are on the wing again. Lehigh was touched long enough to get some supplies and chat with the many people who came to see the canoes and to ask about our starting point, destination, and whether we were " doing it for fun." There was one question which was universally asked : " What do such boats cost ? " Our invariable reply was, " one hundred dollars, fully rigged for sailing, paddling or cruising."

We were off again, leisurely paddling down, on the alert for a good camping place. As the sky was clear and no sign of a thunder storm in the air, a dense forest was chosen, near a deserted house. Supper eaten, tents were being put over the canoes, preparatory to turning in as soon as darkness appeared, when a faint sound came from far down the river, coming nearer, and anon fading away in the distance. As the sound came nearer, it was discovered to be a small pack of fox hounds in full cry. Their owner, who came near us, explained that his hounds had struck the trail of a wolf, as it was supposed, but he had taken them from the trail, as the fur was worthless at this time of year. On account of the flood driving these animals to the high lands, he had caught seven in the last two months. While the sport may be considered somewhat questionable by many people, it would be hard to convince any one who has ever " followed the hounds " that it is not the most exhilarating music in the world. The only gun in camp was double shotted that night. Camp axes were placed in easy reach and the canoeists slept on their arms, so to speak.

Passing the mouth of the Boone River, we asked a man who was herding cattle some questions in regard to the locality, which he answered very politely, after which he whipped up his mule and rode down the river bank at a rate of speed usually acquired by those " going for a doctor " in an urgent case. The cause of his rapid riding was made apparent at the next bend of the river, for he had marshaled his wife, children and mother, to the river bank to see us pass. The canoes were pulled up close to the shore for their inspection and every question answered in detail, and when we bade them a pleasant good day, they watched us until the bend of the river hid us from view.

During the day, we passed a beautiful, rocky cliff of perhaps a mile in length, in the shelter of which, grouped in neighborhoods, were the nests of hundreds of cliff swallows. These nests are built of mud, of a peculiar kind of soil, which seems to adhere to the overhanging rock in so solid a way as to bear the burden of its own weight. the mother and young birds. The nests are built somewhat round. suggestive of a jug, the neck of which turns slightly down, the better to keep out the falling rain. It would puzzle a boy or a girl. I think, to make so complete a house as these patient birds have made without hands and to group them so artistically as they were here placed. I paddled my canoe within a few feet of their nests and the colonists, as they were approached. came out in great swarms, filling the air with their alarmed twitterings. It is likely this was the first time during nesting season they had been disturbed, as the river side of the cliffs was inaccessible except by boat.

We intended lying still in camp all day Sunday, but our supply of ice became exhausted, and we concluded to drop down, quietly, to Moingona for more. It had been a source of amusement to ask of fishermen and others the distance to the next bridge, town or railroad. in order to hear their widely different answers. The most truthful answer, probably, was given by a grave individual who was indulging in a Sunday fish on a shady bank. I asked, " Can you tell me how far it is to Moingona ? " He cleared his throat as he thoughtfully answered, " Damfino." We passed.

Moingona was reached, but not a pound of ice could be had, so we went into camp a short distance below to spend the day quietly. A storm of wind and rain broke upon us at six o'clock, but being well protected by our tents we enjoyed the grateful change of temperature. Soon after, a beautiful rainbow made its appearance, and if such a phenomenon occurred only once in a hundred years and had been well advertised, it would have had an audience of the best and most scientific people of the old and new world.

While there are many beautiful things in nature, there are occasional tragedies in the animal and reptile kingdoms that seldom fall under the observation. On an island, far up the river, there hangs by the neck, in the narrow forks of a willow tree, eighteen feet above the present river surface, a large turtle. How did he get there? The explanation is easy. While swimming down a swift current his head was caught in the forks of a willow, and, slipping down to the narrower part as he struggled for freedom, was held as by a vise. Turtles are very tenacious of life. Perhaps he lived for days, and, as the waters receded, he hung high and dry.

It was only by chance, a yearling calf was discovered, entangled in some roots at a precipitous bank where it had fallen. Its pitiable condition excited our sympathy, and after a little time it was disentangled and urged down the river where the bank was less precipitous and where, after several efforts, it got safely upon solid ground.

On Monday morning, we rose with the lark, as High Bridge was to be reached at three o'clock. We were delayed until nine o'clock in starting. Mr. Weatherly, in trying to get some water for the coffee, trusted to some roots projecting over the river bank, but they proved to be rotten and he fell in twelve feet of water, very pluckily holding on to the coffee pot. I ran to his assistance, rescuing the coffee pot, while he, "grabbing a root," and dripping with coolness, scrambled out, laughing heartily. There was no change of clothing in camp, so there was only one thing for him to do wring out the wet garments, hang them on a line in the sun, and array himself in a big blanket. In consideration of his moist condition, breakfast was served in the broiling hot sun.

Off at last for an easy day's work of thirty-five miles. The river had become more common-place, and yet there were some beautiful forests, rocks and bluffs. The wildness began to wane after Moingona is passed and instead of rocky banks, mud is the general character of all landings.

The bluffs of High Bridge were seen about three o'clock and half an hour later, our canoes were resting under the sugar maple trees of that picturesque spot. The ground was strewn with broken bottles, playing cards and filth of all kinds, and it needed not any description of the Sunday picnic to designate its characteristics the day previous to our arrival.

It seems too bad that so beautiful a spot should be given over to such a debauch and Sabbath desecration. Being hungry for news, not having seen a Des Moines paper for some days, a search was made in the hope that some of the fragments might be found to give a little home news. I succeeded in finding half a Register, well stained with what might have been iced tea, a fragment of beer-stained Leader, and an Iowa Capital complete, well frescoed with custard pie. With these a very pleasant hour was passed.

A storm of wind and rain caught us here, and it was one of the most blissful experiences of the cruise to lie snugly in our cozy little nests and hear the rain patter within a few feet of our faces.

High Bridge is a pretty spot. It is about as pretty as nature can make it. A new steel bridge is soon to take the place of the present one, which will much enhance its beauty and grandeur.

A hearty breakfast was eaten about ten o'clock and preparations for the last day's run was made. The rain still continued at intervals after the start, but with the deck hatches and rubber blankets in place, it mattered but little.

The famous Willow Spring, at Corydon bridge, was a welcome sight; for no thirsty one ever drinks of the water there but remembers its sweetness and purity ever after. The water is free to every passer by and the spring was never known to fail.

From Corydon bridge, it is an easy journey to Des Moines. Soon the river became more familiar. Lawson saw mill, mouth of Beaver, McClelland's mill, Nourse's farm, and now soon the capitol dome, lighted up by the setting sun of the longest day in the year, tells of the cruise so nearly and happily ended. And now. rounding Thompson's bend, a portion of the city bursts on our sight in the rays of the departing god of day.   Home and friends ! The canoes are placed in their accustomed brackets and we tread the noisy streets   ten times more noisy by contrast with a week of quietness, yet with a happiness that even a knowledge of accumulated work piled up before us cannot take out of our hearts.

www.ingramcontent.com/pod-product-compliance
Lightning Source LLC
Chambersburg PA
CBHW020547270326
41927CB00006B/751